# YOUR SOCIAL WORLD EXPLAINED

## SPENCER STERN

**Your Social World Explained**
Copyright © 2016 by Spencer Stern

ISBN-13: 978-1505266641
ISBN-10: 1505266645

# *Preface*

Clueless about how to traverse the social world effectively? Do you need help with your social navigation skills? Why do you not perceive and value things the same way as others? Has anyone ever forced you to do something you did not feel 'right' doing?

These questions and more will get answered as you
- learn about yourself and others;
- discover what psychological type you identify with;
- recognise your natural strengths and weaknesses;
- identify practical ways for personal growth;
- learn what makes you different from the other types;

Once you know all this it will take an enormous weight off your shoulders.

Knowing others will allow you to see things from their perspective, which will increase understanding and help reduce conflicts. The reasons for this will get clearer as you read this book. It has to do with your brain. Moreover, once you learn these reasons, you will never have to feel guilty about your true self ever again.

You will learn about relationships and why you may get along with certain people and why you cannot seem to get along with other people no matter how hard you try.

I wrote this book because you wanted or needed to have your social navigation skills enhanced to make you more successful, less stressed out, and eventually wise in your network of relationships.

*"Consider the following. We humans are social beings. We come into the world as the result of others' actions. We survive here in dependence on others. Whether we like it or not, there is hardly a moment of our lives when we do not benefit from others' activities. For this reason it is hardly surprising that most of our happiness arises in the context of our relationships with others."*
*— His Holiness the 14th Dalai Lama*

I would like to welcome you to a journey of social discovery where I have combined over ten years knowledge and experience in the exciting field of Socionics. In that time I have visited many related websites, have partaken in on-line debates, and have networked with others who also have a keen interest.

I trust that your social dealings will get better from reading this book.

Let's begin!

## TABLE OF CONTENTS

# INTRODUCTION

*"Today the network of relationships linking the human race to itself and to the rest of the biosphere is so complex that all aspects affect all others to an extraordinary degree. Someone should be studying the whole system, however crudely that has to be done, because no gluing together of partial studies of a complex non-linear system can give a good idea of the behaviour of the whole."*
*– Murray Gell-Mann (1997)*

The empirical evidence for this book appears to me as "all around us" such as in the workplace, in families, etc. How we react to each other and why certain ways of thinking upset or arouse others can now seem more comprehensible to all.

The research contained within this book will have potential applications for:
- Career guidance;
- Personal development;
- Corporate recruitment;
- Relationship counselling;
- Psychoanalysis/therapy;
- Learning requirements/Pedagogy;
- Matchmaking/Networking;

Navigating the social world comes through a strong understanding of some key terms described below:
- Socion, defined as either a full set of the sixteen types brought together, or the sixteen inter-type interactions between them. A word that can only mean "the social sphere" about the sixteen types as a whole, or just put the entire "social system".
- Quadra, defined as a particular grouping of psychological types that share a feeling of comfort, security, confidence and understanding. Each member may gain feelings of psychotherapeutic and physical comfort, full understanding and emotional satisfaction. An important concept to

understand because it shows how four types out of sixteen have similar world-views and motivational outlooks.

In proceeding chapters, I will present the various psychological types arranged by Quadra, which in turn represents a structural unit of the Socion. The analysis of the Socion will derive from academic knowledge of Socionics and actual experiences together with how specific types act similar or different from each other in distinct ways.

Later on, we will look at the social dynamics between psychological types in more depth exploring how particular types of relationship may come across to us as more or less favourable than others in a given situation.

As you will likely discover, no 'good' or 'bad' type exists per se although, with sixteen unique ways of interpreting and metabolising information about the world around us, some will no doubt have a unique advantage in particular situations. Each psychological type has specific 'little' and 'big' strengths to make use of in the right context with others.

A population census measuring the distribution of psychological types may reveal that some seem to exist more abundantly than others and with good reason as I will now explain.

Somehow or other, society appears to have the right amount of what it needs regarding psychological types. For example, it may require two active thinkers with five able doers to complete the task of designing and building a bridge across a lake. This equates to the makings of a corporation whereby a group of people get assembled for the purpose of bringing an idea into reality through teamwork.

Hopefully, you will realise that associating yourself with a psychological type does not ultimately define you since your unique character allows you to override it necessarily. A constant "balancing act" then arises between asserting your uniqueness and acting in alignment with your hard wired psyche and resulting behaviours.

Typology, the study and classification of individuals into "types", provides the perspective to understand your behaviour, habits and interpretation of the world, which in turn helps your self-discovery. I found that an appreciation for psychological types remains a useful tool for nurturing personal development and facilitating better social world understanding.

This book equates to my unique interpretation of Socionics whereby I have derived the core concepts and developed them further to make them more intuitive. Since Socionics itself approximates to a "decentralised field of study" there remains ample room for further discussion and modernising of this theorem.

Before we move onto the next section, I thought it worth mentioning that Socionics sometimes gets labelled as a "pseudo-science" perhaps by those who prefer to avoid modelling human behaviour and psychology in-depth. I believe however that with recent advances in cognitive research and neuroscience there lies a great opportunity to test the predictions made by Socionics. I, therefore, consider Socionics as a 'young but emerging science' in need of further research. I would kindly ask you, the reader, to examine this book carefully with an open mind, and see where it takes you in better understanding yourself and those around you.

## A HISTORY OF SOCIONICS

Aušra Augustinavičiūtė (also credited as Aushra Augusta), a Lithuanian psychologist was born in the year 1927, died aged 78 in 2005 and authored numerous scientific theories and discoveries - the founder of Socionics.

Aushra integrated Freud's 'structural theory', Jung's Psychological Types and Kępiński's theory of 'informational metabolism' to create Socionics, a new theory and model of the psyche that describes the development of relations between types.

According to this theory, a personality type exists within a "dyad" with one other type. A "quadra" represents four personality types that portray informational dynamics important for small groups. In turn, quadras can join to form a "socion" of 16 distinct personality types.

Let's now explore a bit more in-depth those previous works that gave rise to the field of Socionics.

### Sigmund Freud

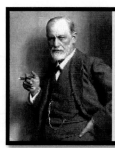

Sigmund Freud (1856-1939) was an Austrian neurologist who founded the psychoanalytic school of psychiatry. He is considered the father of psychoanalysis.

Freud is considered one of the most prominent thinkers of the first half of the 20th century, in terms of originality and intellectual influence.

Socionics integrates Freud's 'structural theory' which claims that the psyche has divisions known as ego, super-ego and id. In brief, the id contains 'primitive desires' (hunger, rage, and sex), the super-ego contains internalised norms, morality and taboos, and the ego mediates between the two and may include or give rise to the sense of self.

According to Freud's early writings, the ego represents a sense of self; he later began to portray it more as a set of psychic functions such as reality-testing, defence, synthesis of information, intellectual functioning, and memory. He also asserted that the super-ego acts as the conscience, maintaining our sense of morality and the prevention of taboos. Lastly, the id appeared to him as "the reservoir of need-gratification impulses" such as the primitive instinctual drives of sexuality and aggression.

### Carl Jung

Carl Jung (1875 - 1961) was a Swiss psychiatrist. Founder of a neopsychoanalytic school of psychology, which he named Analytical Psychology.

Jung's unique and broadly influential approach to psychology has emphasized understanding the psyche through exploring the worlds of dreams, art, mythology, world religion and philosophy.

Socionics integrates Jung's "theory of psychological types" which essentially says that we experience the world in four primary modes. In Jung's model we have two rational functions (thinking and feeling), and two perceptive functions (sensation and intuition). According to Jung, sensation and intuition represent the perception of facts and perception of the unseen respectively. He also asserted that thinking and feeling approximates with analytical, deductive cognition and synthetic, all-inclusive cognition respectively.

Lastly, a subdivision exists for each function between what Jung identified as 'introversion' and 'extroversion'. The often misunderstood terms 'extrovert' and 'introvert' derive from this work and in my view have befallen into words used as stereotypes. In Jung's original usage, however, the extrovert orientation finds meaning outside the self, in the surrounding world, whereas the introvert goes introspective and finds it from within. When correctly associated this would apply to an individual's functions rather than a generalised judgement of the personality as a whole. For example, people who may show characteristics of introversion do not necessarily equate to having a social problem that needs 'curing' per se.

## Antoni Kępiński

Antoni Kepinski (1918 - 1972) was a Polish psychiatrist. His books :
* Psychopatologia nerwic (Psychopathology of neuroses)
* Schizofrenia (Schizophrenia)
* Melancholia (Melancholy)
* Psychopatie (Psychopathologies)
* Lek (Fear)
* Podstawowe zagadnienia wspolczesnej psychiatrii
* Poznanie chorego
* Rytm zycia (The Rhythm of Life)

Socionics integrates this Kępiński's "information metabolism" theory of human social interactions that explains how information gets processed by individuals. Psychological features such as 'attention', 'interests', 'memory' and 'motivation' reflect the components of this theory which seem to develop upon an analogy close to 'energy metabolism'.

According to this analogy, information that arrives as signals from outside an organism follow the same pattern as food which would provide the source material for energy metabolism. To Kępiński the brain, therefore, represented the key information metabolism system.

## PSYCHE OVERVIEW

To understand the psyche in Socionics we have a model of the mind aptly named "Model A" where the 'A' represents the initial from the name of the founder, an embodiment of Augusta, who created it. The model itself describes the three top works of Freud, Jung and Kępiński merged into one where:

1. Freud's structural theory provides the backbone of the Model A.
2. Jung's work on cognitive functions provides the information elements inserted into the Model A.
3. Kępiński's information metabolism theory provides the necessary rules for where the elements get placed in the Model A.

### MODEL A (ORIGINAL)

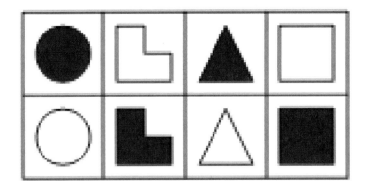

The Model A (above) has remained relatively simple since it got conceived back in the 1970's. It usually gets presented in a simple matrix grid with black (extroverted) and white (introverted) symbols of the information elements. To the untrained eye, it probably means little or nothing but to the Socionics expert it depicts a particular psychological type's ordering of the eight information elements.

I have pioneered an extended Model A to present the original better with intuitive features as you will see next.

## Model A (Extended)

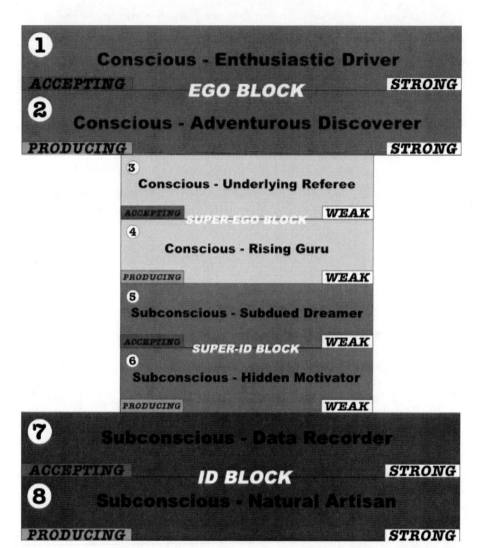

### Explanation of the Model A (Extended)

Let us now imagine that the psyche makes up the layers of an onion. The first four layers comprise of the conscious part of the psyche (ego and super-ego) and the next four make up the subconscious (super-id and id).

So we have a psyche model where:

- The first two layers make up your ego, in other words, the most certain and strongest aspects of your personality. It contains the least amount of shyness.
- The third and fourth layers make up your superego, the internal conscience behind your ego. This can seem like your source of social anxiety and doubt.
- The fifth and sixth layers make up your super-id, the internal conscience behind the id. This represents the origin of your childishness and suggestibility.
- The seventh and eighth layers make up your id, your aggressive and most instinctual self. This mostly contains your hidden strengths that you may not even know you have.

Furthermore, you would have noticed that each block has relative strengths and directions for the places where the information elements will go, where:

- The first, second, seventh and eighth attitudes have strong domination i.e. confidently used with a large amount of information that may influence others and the surroundings in a certain way.
- The third, fourth, fifth and sixth attitudes have weak domination i.e. not confidently used with an insufficient amount of information and may remain subject to the influence of others.
- The odd numbered attitudes (1, 3, 5, and 7) have accepting orientation i.e. an INPUT or scanning function whereby your brain takes a snapshot of reality and acquires it.
- The even numbered attitudes (2, 4, 6, and 8) have producing orientation i.e. an OUTPUT or creative function whereby your brain does something productive because of how the information is taken in previously.
- The first four attitudes (1, 2, 3, and 4) make conscious effort i.e. an individual analyses a certain aspect of reality consciously and strives to verbalise it.
- The last four attitudes (5, 6, 7, and 8) make subconscious effort i.e. an individual studies a certain aspect of reality

subconsciously – subjectively or "through oneself" through hands-on contact.

## CORRESPONDING BLOCKS

I shall now digress for a moment from the Model A (extended) where I have a side model that depicts the four corresponding blocks (or pairs of the personality).

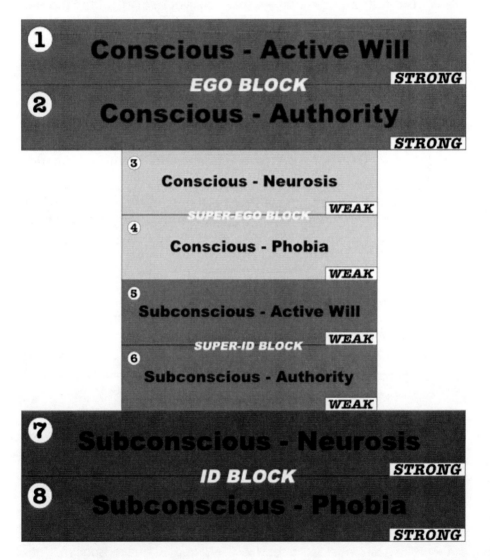

Let us now imagine that the ordering of the psyche goes a bit like a family going on a road-trip in a car, where:

- The first and fifth functions form your active will or strength of character. This represents to me the person who drives the car.
- The second and sixth functions form your authority or key influences behind your active will. This would seem to me like the person sitting alongside the driver in the passenger seat acting as navigator and aiding in decision-making.
- The third and seventh functions form your area of neurosis or the anxiety/hang-ups you may have, related to the dominance of your active will and authority. This would seem to me like a child in the back of the car coming along for the ride with little or no say on where they are heading.
- The fourth and eighth functions form your area of phobia or the fears/timidity you may have, related to the dominance of your active will and authority. This would seem to me like a baby strapped into a baby seat in the back with a poor ability to assert what they want (apart from crying of course) and thus goes relatively unnoticed and misunderstood.

By now it should seem obvious where Freud's original concept of the Ego, Super-Ego and Id come into play.

Socionics added the idea of the Super-Id (the conscience behind the Id). I like to think of this as your personality's "super kid" whereby it represents to me the "zone of childishness and suggestibility". This later gives rise to what you likely seek to find in the social world that another type can fulfil. More on that, later.

## JUNGIAN FUNCTIONS

According to Carl Jung's work entitled "Psychological Types" there equates to four basic cognitive functions, where two operate rationally, and the other two behave irrationally, as follows:

- Rational:
    - Feeling
    - Thinking
- Irrational:
    - Sensing
    - Intuition

In Socionics, Feeling and Thinking translate respectively as Ethics and Logic. This may alleviate some confusion whereby a person with strong ethics does not necessarily experience strong feelings towards others as such. Each cognitive function then gets subdivided further into either Introverted or Extroverted providing a total of eight functions.

The technical nature of Socionics does not easily allow the non-expert to understand what these terms mean when correctly applied to a personality type's individual psyche model. Therefore I have re-imagined these internal cognitive functions as "attitudes" which I believe has a better connotation for practical purposes. In other words, rather than focus on "internal names" that only a Socionics expert would perhaps understand fully I have considered new "external names" that the rest of us can better understand.

In the following diagram, I have painstakingly translated the internal function names into external attitude names because I believe we all want to know how they manifest in reality. In just two word descriptors I have summarised what could take months, even years, to fully grasp properly.

| Internal Functions | | External Attitudes | |
|---|---|---|---|
| Introverted Sensing | ○ | Dynamic Stabilization | |
| Extroverted Sensing | ● | Tactical Action | |
| Introverted Intuition | △ | Reality Distillation | |
| Extroverted Intuition | ▲ | Creative Thinking | |
| Introverted Ethics | ⌐ | Ethical Harmony | |
| Extroverted Ethics | ⌐ | Social Interest | |
| Introverted Logic | □ | Academic Knowledge | |
| Extroverted Logic | ■ | Practical Results | |

Interestingly while each of these attitudes can have their definition on their own, they can take on a new significance depending on where they reside in the Model A. For example, what does Ethical Harmony (Introverted Ethics) mean when a person's psychological type has it as their first attitude or the third?

We'll get to that as you begin to read about each type and how their psyche changes depending on where these function/attitudes got placed into the Model A.

I now present my short and succinct descriptions of what I will now refer to as "the eight attitudes":

- Dynamic Stabilization represents to me the anchoring of one's self to "safe bets" in a world that may come across as inherently irrational or chaotic.
- Tactical Action represents to me the act of living life at the moment and accepting the world with a 'just react' response.

- Reality Distillation represents to me the art of seeing through the distortions that reality creates, the ability of just knowing or having hunches of unfounded truth and the source of unknown ideas.
- Creative Thinking represents to me the process of noticing the trends and possibilities in the world that inherently contains a wealth of unknown opportunities yet for one to find and exploit.
- Ethical Harmony represents to me the concern about the harmony between self and others where everyone has a unique soul and the rational attitude of upholding moral values.
- Social Interest represents to me the concern one has about the roles other people play about one another and how we all relate to a socially shared world.
- Academic Knowledge represents to me the attitude of seeking to understand how something works structurally, demanding complete and complex underlying knowledge.
- Practical Results represents to me the attitude of seeking to obtain practical and externally predictable results through decisive decision-making.

These external attitudes derived from internal functions will begin to make more sense in the context of the sixteen types as we see how they might manifest themselves in the social world.

## THE PRINCIPLES BEHIND THE SIXTEEN TYPES

You may wonder and ask where we get this number of sixteen. The eight attitudes have many possible combinations in the Model A although we only get sixteen psychological types based on the following rules, as paraphrased from Socionics research itself:

- Each and every information element must appear in the model once;
- The conscious and subconscious must consist of either all static elements or all dynamic elements;
  - Static elements include Tactical Action, Creative Thinking, Academic Knowledge, and Ethical Harmony.

- Static elements perceive reality in a fixed style i.e. they observe the environment over time as-is without a change of opinion.
  - Dynamic elements include Dynamic Stabilization, Reality Distillation, Practical Results, and Social Interest.
    - Dynamic elements perceive reality in a variable style i.e. they observe the environment over time with consistently evolving judgements.
- The accepting and producing attitudes must contain either all rational or all irrational elements;
- Each block must consist of one extroverted and one introverted element;
- The subconscious must mirror the conscious with elements of opposite orientation;

The only valid subtypes that I know of equate to saying that we have sixteen male and sixteen female types where differences in gender produce even more discussion with regards to psychological type.

## MODEL A POSITIONAL DESCRIPTIONS

Now that we've looked at the Model A in both a classical and modern interpretation I find it fitting to explain each of the various positions and what they will ultimately mean when we begin placing information elements in them later on.

From the egotistical areas of the psyche through to the conscientious, suggestible and aggressive you'll begin to notice why perhaps you and others act the way they do. The question remains to discover the attitudes that govern behaviour in totality.

Let us now see how the underlying power behind understanding the Model A. You may like to refer to the previous diagrams as a visual reminder as we delve deeper into the psyche.

## 1) ENTHUSIASTIC DRIVER [STRONG & ACCEPTING]

The first attitude represents to me the strongest and most conscious part of the psyche. It forms the core of one's perceptions of reality, perceiving information with the greatest clarity and level of detail. One has near photographic memory of everything consciously registered or processed using one's first attitude.

The first attitude may become subject to the "mind projection fallacy", a term coined by philosopher E. T. Jaynes, whereby the perception of reality from one's first attitude may indeed equate to one's ignorance and not represent 'true reality'. Hence, the 'view of reality' from two identical types can seem different.

The first attitude constantly observes and studies reality. This information element or attitude views reality as an objective component. It believes that everyone should have access to its knowledge base.

The individual knows how to obtain authoritative information related to his first attitude and how to get this kind of information out to other people.

One tries to become a specialist in areas relating to one's first attitude and finds the best standards to promote. The first attitude always has its distinct sphere of interests.

Individuals do not shy about demonstrating their first attitude or receiving criticism about what they do or think using their first attitude. One's first attitude tends to value most in oneself. It becomes the core of one's identity. They also think little of criticising others from the standpoint of their first attitude.

In one's opinions and activities related to one's first attitude one rarely yields to others' influence and can more than capable of standing up for one's self and leading others to it. The first attitude has an interest in others just as much or more than oneself and needs a large field to apply itself.

It needs people that will heed it's qualified advice and accept it's program.

## 2) ADVENTUROUS DISCOVERER [STRONG & PRODUCING]

The second attitude represents to me the psyche's next most conscious attitude after the first. The individual uses it as a tool to achieve one's goals related to one's first attitude and perceives this aspect of reality as a means, not an end.

By honing this tool to serve the first attitude's demands, one discovers or invents something new or previously unknown.

One prefers to create one's new version of things relating to one's second attitude rather than dig through old material that one does not try hard to remember.

Individuals view their second attitude more as their personal skill or quality than as an objective component of reality.
Hence, criticism probably seems more unpleasant than for the first attitude. At the same time, when others need our help using our second attitude we help with pleasure and enthusiasm.

One believes that everyone should have the right to freedom and creativity in this aspect of reality. If no one needs our help in this aspect of reality, we feel unneeded. The more those around us need our expertise in this area, the greater our self-actualization in society.

## 3) UNDERLYING REFEREE [WEAK & ACCEPTING]

The third attitude receives less attention than the first two and accumulates information periodically. One doesn't completely know whether they perceive things accurately with it or not, and their memory of things doesn't hold well.

There would seem like not always enough information available about this aspect of reality even for the individual himself to get by. The third attitude does not have its distinct sphere of interests; almost any information out of the norm can interest the individual.

When making decisions about this aspect of reality the individual hesitates and doubts himself trying to get advice from others if he can if others will treat him respectfully in this regard. The third attitude may seem quite sensitive to criticism and tries not to criticise or impose on others.

Since the weak attitude in this position finds it difficult to withstand or counter other peoples' views about this aspect of reality, individuals try to meet accepted standards and attempt to become at least average in this area. If they do make mistakes, they usually feel bad that others have not taught them to do better.

In this area, a person can give advice based on what they have heard from others but doesn't act too unsure of their self to help. The third attitude needs others to help without making a big deal of it.

One needs to have someone who can sympathise to discuss issues relating to this attitude and approve one's decisions. In this case, the individual becomes much more self-assured and secure and begins to live more fully.

Also, this third attitude gradually becomes an encyclopaedia of useful information, which others can derive value. The calmer and more secure one acts about everything relating to one's third attitude and the more attention one gives it, the greater one's success.

However, the third attitude rarely gets as categorical and forceful as the first and can never rise to the same heights of vision. At its best development, it remains a practical instrument to serve the interests of the individual and those immediately surrounding him.

### 4) RISING GURU [WEAK & PRODUCING]
The fourth attitude represents to me the weakest of the conscious attitudes. It perceives information superficially at best. The third attitude provides it with little information for making confident judgements and decisions. It finds it very difficult to withstand pressure from others.

Pressure or excessive information related to this aspect of reality can cause a multitude of complexes, neuroses, and unhealthy reactions to one's surroundings (self-flagellation to arouse pity, imagining things that do not exist, etc.).

The individual tries not to interfere in other's business (unless it directly affects him) and does not like people who come across as curious or pushy in this aspect of reality. Discussion of these things in this aspect remains possible only if one raises the subject oneself.

Any excessive attention given to these things sets one on guard – even compliments (unless one knows of the other's sincerity).

One tends to blow failures and criticism (real or perceived) of their fourth attitude out of proportion and may mull over them for days, causing a sort of mental paralysis and lengthy self-re-evaluation.

The fourth attitude has difficulty understanding and remembering information and tends to resort to generalisations that manifest as often primitive and lopsided. One's fourth attitude gets especially sensitive to criticism and requires tactful concern from others, not criticism.

What one's fourth attitude needs approximates to freedom of manifestation without outside commentary. It especially needs a friend to depend on who has an opinion on this aspect of reality.

Otherwise, steady "attacks" on this attitude can turn life into a prison where one feels constantly watched and judged.

## 5) SUBDUED DREAMER [WEAK & ACCEPTING]
The fifth attitude has great difficulty making sense of information on its own. Information perceived on the one hand, as little understood background noise and on the other hand as something of great importance.
The individual feels good when others explain to him what he experiences in this aspect of reality and what he should do about it.

One's opinions in this area may find themselves easily influenced. Without others' care and concern, one feels like an abandoned child. A person rarely feels ashamed about problems related to his fifth attitude and can easily request help if he sees that others are self-assured in this area.

If others speak in an authoritative tone, one listens carefully to advice having to do with one's fifth attitude. One rarely stands up for the fifth attitude's interests, but accepts as much help as others are willing to give. Criticism from others may interpret itself as concern for one's needs.

Self-perfection on one's own does not come easy and remains extremely difficult. If the individual has someone he trusts to follow, he feels happy and protected. Otherwise, he feels resentful of society for not providing him with the care and assistance he needs.

## 6) HIDDEN MOTIVATOR [WEAK & PRODUCING]
The sixth attitude represents the part of the psyche where one's instinctive reactions to signals coming from the fifth attitude form. This area provides a person with the least conscious freedom. One does not know the state of one's sixth attitude.

Criticism may seem unpleasant and arouses responses like "either help me or keep your mouth shut." An individual tries to liquidate any negative influences that make it harder for the sixth attitude to operate.
On the other hand, praise of one's sixth attitude makes for the best compliment possible. Any help and concern in this area a person can seem openly grateful for and tries to reciprocate. Any malfunctions or maladjustment of the sixth attitude seriously impairs the psyche's operation.

## 7) DATA RECORDER [STRONG & ACCEPTING]
The seventh attitude will keenly observe and remember important information, which may produce opinions or behaviour that may come across as aggressive or arrogant. This attitude does not create but adheres to observed behaviour.

**8) NATURAL ARTISAN [STRONG & PRODUCING]**
The eighth attitude automatically works for you and helps others. You don't typically know about this attitude as a skill.

**And So It Begins**
Depending on which attitude you have in specific places in the Model A, you should find it easier to understand:

- Why you do well at some things where to say a strong Enthusiastic Driver attitude of Academic Knowledge may manifest itself as a need to understand anything of interest and of course not shy away from talking about it.
- Why you may avoid certain things where to say a weak Rising Guru attitude of Tactical Action may manifest itself as a weak desire to get things done in a practical matter.
- What you may need help with where says a weak Subdued Dreamer attitude of Social Interest may manifest itself as a naive understanding of what to expect or do in a social environment.
- What you can help others with where to say a strong Natural Artisan attitude of Reality Distillation may manifest itself unassumingly as an ability to weed through superfluous details in a conversation.

This knowledge has changed the way I look at people and the social world. A wonderful thing because it provided me with insights into human behaviour which I now share with you. I also noted that specific strong and weak attitudes will likely have manifested behaviours and mannerisms that should now seem more understandable and recognisable.

In the next chapter that follows we begin to see how sixteen distinct natures come about due to structural differences of the psyche. As you take the following psychological type test and read the profiles, it may become apparent that your identified type may differ in significant ways. Don't concern yourself about this. Remember, I wrote this book to serve as a guide and tool and cannot account for your individual life experiences. For example, an introverted type may by circumstances, develop an outgoing persona based on social pressures. As you learn about the various types, you will see how each fit into the 'big picture' socially.

Before we begin exploring the sixteen types, I find it worth mentioning that personality does not equal character. The character represents to me a culmination of your values and can develop in either positive or negative directions depending on many factors and circumstances. It can essentially override your personality although like a bungee rope it can only do so much before your "default self" wants to re-assert itself again.

# QUICK TYPOLOGY TEST

**This brief test helps you to determine your psychological type. For each of the following questions choose the side which most resonates with you to get your four-letter code that will signify your type.**

Instructions: Find your four-letter code by choosing a column as your preferred answer to each question then taking the letter in each curly bracket to construct your type. So for example, if you agreed with all the left columns you would end up with Extrovert {E}, Sensing {S}, Thinking {T}, Perceiving {p} giving you the code "ESTp".

Please note: This quick test may not reveal your true psychological type straight away. In fact, it may give a completely inaccurate answer and so further reading of the upcoming profiles in this book will help to verify and confirm it. In fact, I've written this book in such a manner that the only true way to know your type would seem to me as to know all the other types equally, similar to the idea behind the following quotation from Laozi.

> *"Knowing others is intelligence; knowing yourself is true wisdom. Mastering others is strength; mastering yourself is true power. If you realize that you have enough, you are truly rich."*
>
> — *Laozi, Tao Te Ching*

Let's get to the first question!

## QUESTION 1: HOW DO YOU DIRECT YOUR SOCIAL ENERGIES?

| Extroverts {E} | Introverts {I} |
| --- | --- |
| • You prefer to have people around you than your own thoughts and feelings.<br>• You often seem talkative bouncing your opinions off and with others.<br>• You like taking action and generally showing initiative.<br>• You easily make new friends or adapt to new groups of people.<br>• You generally say what you think rather than keeping your thoughts to yourself.<br>• You take a keen interest in new people and can easily break unwanted relations. | • You prefer your own thoughts and feelings than people around you.<br>• You feel a need to have your own territory or space away from others.<br>• You often appear reserved, quiet and low-key.<br>• You probably do not have many friends except for a few close ones.<br>• You generally have difficulty making new contacts.<br>• You do not like unexpected visits and usually work well alone. |

Quick Answer Tip: Think about a typical social situation where you don't know anyone (yet). Do you greet with a smile and enthusiasm or keep your head low and barely speak a whisper? Do you spend most of your time alone or with people?

## QUESTION 2: HOW DO YOU INTERPRET YOUR SURROUNDINGS?

| Sensing Types {S} | Intuitive Types {N} |
| --- | --- |
| • You tend to see everyone, sense everything and live in the here and now.<br>• You can quickly adapt to any situation also liking pleasures based on physical sensation.<br>• You act practical, active, realistic, and self-confident.<br>• You like doing things in a systematic and methodical fashion. | • You tend to live mostly in the past or the future thus worry about it more than the present moment.<br>• You seem interested in everything new and unusual thus disliking routine.<br>• You act idealistic attracted more to the theory than the practice of things.<br>• You like looking at the "big picture." |

Quick Answer Tip: Think about your dress sense for example. Do you wear fashionable clothes often that feel comfortable, or one's that merely serve the function of covering up? Do you spend more time looking after your body or your mind?

## QUESTION 3: HOW DO YOU REASON THE WORLD?

| Thinking Types {T} | Feeling Types {F} |
|---|---|
| • You have an interest in systems, structures, patterns, and exposing everything to logical analysis.<br>• You may seem relatively cold and unemotional evaluating things by your intellect i.e. right or wrong.<br>• You do not like talking about feelings and like to discuss issues logically. | • You seem more interested in people and their feelings, easily passing on your mood to others.<br>• You pay great attention to love and passion evaluating things by ethics i.e. good or bad.<br>• You can get touchy at times or use emotional manipulations, often giving compliments simply to please people. |

Quick Answer Tip: Think about your problem-solving skills. Do you get emotional or keep a cool head when trying to solve problems? Do you act like a "man from Mars" or a "woman from Venus" (regardless of your gender) when it comes to solving problems?

## QUESTION 4: HOW DO YOU ORGANIZE YOUR TIME?

| Perceiving Types {p} | Judging Types {j} |
|---|---|
| • You act impulsively following a situation and can start many things at once without finishing them properly.<br>• You prefer to have freedom from obligations and would rather have a fresh look at things.<br>• Your work productivity depends on your mood and you can often act without any preparation. | • You do not like to leave unanswered questions and tend to plan work ahead in order to finish it.<br>• You do not like to change your decisions once made.<br>• You have a relatively stable work-flow and can easily follow rules and discipline. |

Quick Answer Tip: Think about your punctuality to meetings. Do you keep a firm eye on the clock whether early or late? Do you get a subtle worry or not about getting somewhere on time?

### Let's move forward

You may have at this point determined your psychological type and although you may wish to 'dive in' to reading about your particular type I believe you will derive the most value from this book by learning about all the sixteen types. For example, while each type may stand out on their own they still form part of a social system, which you should understand in its entirety. As you read up on the Socion next, you will notice that the discussion surrounding the external cognitive attitudes will repeat in varying contexts.

At the end of each type profile, I have made a short expostulation on the issues surrounding their personal development. Some ideas will repeat in varying contexts because some types have similarities to others and thus have congruent issues. For example, the analyst and critic with their quasi-identity relations share challenges in their mental capacities to turn ideas into reality.

# PART ONE: THE SOCION

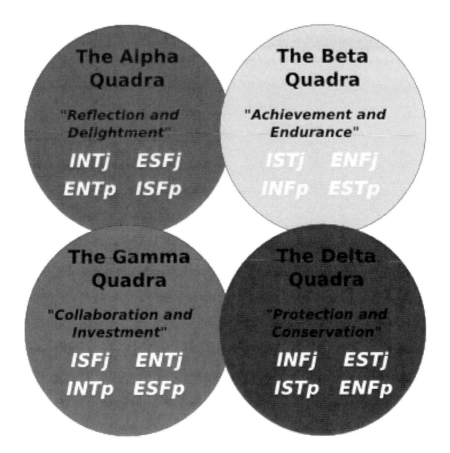

Quadras represent to me a profound exposé and classification of social units. A single Quadra makes up a structural unit of the socion and acts as the chief 'umbrella' small group that organises psychological types together that share similar values, motivations and outlooks on life.

For now, however, I present a set of entertaining introductions to the sixteen psychological types complete with their attitude analyses, which will get to the root of their personal and outward behaviours.

As you can probably see at a glance, the four quadras have a particular contribution to society which we will now explore in turn proceeded by the members they each contain.

# THE ALPHA QUADRA

Summary:
- Intellectual Age: Pre-Adolescence with Child-Like Curiosities.
- Group Mantra: "Constant and Never-Ending Personal & Social Improvement".
- Driving Motivation: Individualistic Capitalism.
- Typical Behaviours: Spontaneous, Lighthearted, and Trivial.
- Social Role: Renaissance Men & Women Whom Bring New Ideas and Information into The Socion.
- Political Philosophy: Strong Individualism aka "Federation of Individuals". Libertarian views.
- Epistemology: Gnosticism, Idealism, Conceptual Knowledge.
- Moral Dilemma: "Why can't we serve and rule no-one allowing us to work towards creative values for self and society?"

Members:
- The "INTj" Analyst
- The "ESFj" Enthusiast
- The "ENTp" Searcher
- The "ISFp" Mediator

A combination of NT's and SF's which translates to "Young Scientists" and "Networking Socialisers" whom together form, in a nutshell, society's Research & Development division. The kind of people who want to network and develop cutting-edge ideas for the rest of the Socion.

## THE "INTJ" ANALYST

### OVERVIEW

The INTj "Analyst" represents to me "the thought leader" who prefers to stay away from the public eye. He has the talent for piecing together the ins and outs of complex systems. He does so where others do not have the time or patience for logical deliberations.

Analysts aim to find a niche that aligns with their traits. They wish to get the most out of their history. They want to fit in their experiences and harness their talents. Their goals when met represent a sense of individual triumph. They like to maintain their freedom.

Analysts have the skill to see social trends. This allows them to thrive in the various societies they come upon. As ascetic people, they cannot always appreciate the beauty of real life. Thus, they prefer to seek out like-minded souls for guidance.

Analysts delight in sponsoring themselves and others in constant growth. They can turn ideas into reality. They do this through deep introspection. They can figure out the upgrades necessary to cause a significant change in the end.

Analysts see paths for growth in many areas. They can notice problems in any scheme of interest. With no trouble at all, they know what currently seems useless to them. They will make thoughtful remarks. They tend to remain discontent with the status quo. They do not like those who do not embrace change.

Analysts mostly have a look of self-control. They have the skill to detach from and make critical analyses of any situation. They tend to have clear thoughts. They take pleasure in building abstract models.

## MODEL A: THE "INTJ" ANALYST

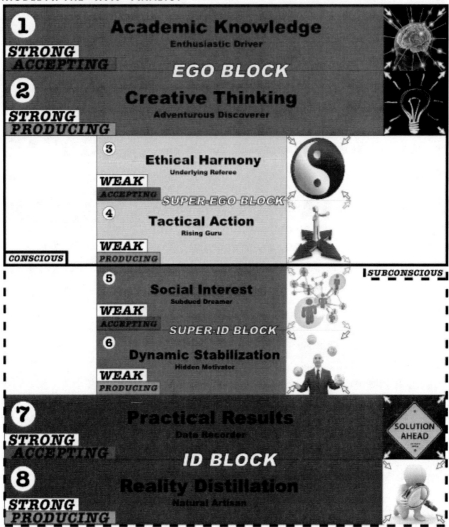

### ATTITUDE ANALYSIS: EGO BLOCK

1. ENTHUSIASTIC DRIVER - ACADEMIC KNOWLEDGE (AK)
"...ALWAYS ADDING NEW TRUTHS..."

Academic Knowledge is the rational first attitude. It leads the analyst to relate whatever he finds himself doing to some larger principles that he may have known in the past. Therefore, AK is like having a kind of mental store of books that describes the inner workings of things. He will refer to his spiritual bookstore a lot when dealing with reality.

Analysts are always adding new truths to their in-house books. To deal with anything it may have to work in unison with the notes recorded in their inner bookstore. When dealing with a new system it may undergo new records. This may seem pointless from an extroverted point of view. Most people do not need to understand how a bicycle works to ride one. They do not have to understand a subject in school if they simply crammed and memorised. They do not have to know how computers work to check their email.

The AK mindset leads the analyst to need full knowledge of whatever takes his interest. He does this in place of looking up the correct procedure. He does not ask friends for their help. He only tries to understand something well enough to use it. In fact, he will try to become the expert on how it works. This kind of understanding takes a lot more time and effort to develop. It can be very flexible once attained. It allows him to deal with aspects of reality that social norms cannot describe.

AK on its own represents highly hidden truths of reality. These insights can be too complicated to put into direct speech. Thus, he has a particular oddness about him. He may confuse others. For example, if he has to make clear a topic with no groundwork.
Hence, AK is a high-bandwidth or deep grasp of the external world. It leads the analyst to try to know the full nature of any system of interest.

## 2. ADVENTUROUS DISCOVERER - CREATIVE THINKING (CT)
"...THE WORLD IS MY OYSTER..."

Creative Thinking is the irrational second attitude. It helps produce insights that the AK mindset needs. Theories go through testing in the real world with trial and error. For example, the analyst walks into a store and asks to check out their most recent camera. The first thing he might do is play with it to build a new updated understanding needed by the AK attitude.

Analysts learn best by free association. In other words, saying or doing what instinctively comes to mind. CT allows them to know what they are doing through live experimentation reinforced with their primary AK attitude. For example, linking what the "play button" does on a mp3 player thus knowing how it works without reading the instructions. In most cases, this results in a quicker grasp of something.

Analysts enjoy their spare time in unusual ways. They at times make the exciting company. For example, at a house party, they decide to awe and inspire others with a sampling of their secret knowledge.

Hence, CT as the second attitude serves as a kind of prompt to the AK attitude that 'the world is my oyster' for research and learning. The CT attitude allows the analyst to see the trends and wealth of potentials. They enjoy a growing understanding of the world around them.

## ATTITUDE ANALYSIS: **SUPER-EGO BLOCK**

### 3. UNDERLYING REFEREE - ETHICAL HARMONY (EH)
"...TO DO THE RIGHT THING..."

Ethical Harmony is the third rational attitude. It is one-half of the super-ego and conscience behind the stronger ego attitudes. For the analyst, inner feelings do not appear on the surface much. Feelings tend to be on behalf of causes that are good, worthy and humane. We may catch a glimpse of it in the unspoken attitude of good will, or the gracious smile or nod. In this sense, we could say that his "actions speak louder than words". It is entirely reasonable for him to project an outward cool demeanour. This gives us a little clue as to his real feelings in any given moment.

Analysts may end up in pointless acts of honour. They could maintain a super self-control or do one's duty like go down with a ship. There is nothing to gain by this directly. They perform this ascetic act to confirm their innate goodness.

As a complex, the analyst may become cross when his ethics are threatened. He expects others to accept his strong sense of reality. He does not want them to pollute it with their often emotion-filled excuses.

Hence, EH as the third attitude leads the analyst to do the right thing in most places. For example, he will more often than not avoid conflicts with others.

## 4. RISING GURU - TACTICAL ACTION (TA)
### "...THE TRUE LATE STARTER..."

Tactical Action is the fourth irrational attitude. It is the conscience behind the stronger ego attitudes. As the producing attitude for the EH attitude, it is the weak desire to accept the world as-is. The analyst will avoid living life in the present. He will prefer to keep his long-range forecasting skills.

As a phobic mindset, this explains why analysts can forget to balance work and play. This can easily lead them to a starvation of their senses. They end up as the true late starter in the context of sensation seeking. Thus, they are usually austere with a refrain from sensual bliss. On the other hand, this withdraws them to focus on their strategic insights without ending up in the drama of life itself.

Hence, TA is a timid attitude for the analyst. It results in a lack of need to enjoy life as-is. With a weak need to respond to nature in the moment, they may miss chances to get things done. Also, they will not seem to live with both feet on the ground.

## ATTITUDE ANALYSIS: SUPER-ID BLOCK

## 5. SUBDUED DREAMER - SOCIAL INTEREST (SI)
### "...THE INNER NEED TO RELATE TO OTHERS..."

Social Interest is the fifth rational attitude. It is one-half of the super-id, the conscience of the id. For the analyst, this mindset is restless in appreciating the roles we all play. The conscious attitudes have sought to know the world through many associations. The SI attitude equates to the inner need to relate to others. For example, at a party, there is a naïve need to make friends.

This swayable attitude may not ask for help in its secret wish to get on with others. For example, building their social network would not seem to them as a huge priority.

Hence, SI is a dormant attitude that wants the analyst to associate more with others. A person with a strong conscious SI attitude can provoke a restart of this desire.

## 6. HIDDEN MOTIVATOR - DYNAMIC STABILIZATION (DS)
### "...THE WORLD IS HECTIC..."

Dynamic Stabilization is the sixth irrational attitude. It is the second half of the super-id, the conscience of the id. For the analyst, it yields results of the SI attitude by fixing them to the known. This attitude does not judge reality well until helped by someone with DS as a conscious attitude.

As the hidden agenda of the analyst, they may like to bring order out of the apparent chaos of reality. They may need help with this weak area of their subconscious mind.

Hence, DS is the weak attitude that the world is hectic full of ever-changing stimuli. For example, the analyst does not go out a lot since they would rather remain out of harm's way.

## ATTITUDE ANALYSIS: ID BLOCK

## 7. DATA RECORDER - PRACTICAL RESULTS (PR)
### "...TO DO SOMETHING PRACTICAL..."

Practical Results is the seventh rational attitude. It is one-half of the id, the most instinctual self. As we delve into the core of the analyst's mind, we find concern for decisive thoughts. The PR mindset will fulfil itself under periods of stress or upset. For example, they lose their job and decide to start their own business.

Hence, PR is a strong subconscious mindset that provides the analyst on a whim to do something practical. They may become an entrepreneur with the right kind of support.

## 8. Natural Artisan - Reality Distillation (RD)
### "...an automatic zest for core truths..."

Reality Distillation is the irrational eighth attitude. It is the second half of the id, the most instinctual self. At the core of the analyst's mind, we find an automatic zest for core truths. Any details, in reality, they deem as extra will go through a sorting process. This attitude keeps them fixed to the crux of what matters.

Hence, RD is a strong subconscious mindset that keeps the analyst on guard against the flaws present in reality. Therefore, they know when others are trying to probe, deceive or otherwise manipulate him.

### Personal Development for INTj's

Analysts tend to gather and share their research data. This can make them come across as big-headed. They enjoy talking their talk. They do not always walk their talk. I suggest that they unite with others to get things done.

Analysts tend to market their work under private brands. They enjoy the sense of self from their work. They do not value others prying into their work. I suggest that they capitalise on their ideas with the aid of others. They need to start evaluating the corporate entity as a vehicle they can use to build wealth.

Analysts more often than not remain locked inside their minds. They are prone to zoning out with their thoughts. They do not have a here and now focus on their work. I suggest that they do more keep fit classes. This will help to ground them to induce more focus.

### Famous Examples of INTj's
- Carl Jung (Swiss Psychiatrist)
- René Descartes (French Philosopher)
- Sigourney Weaver (American Actress)
- George Lucas (American Film Producer)

## THE "ESFJ" ENTHUSIAST

### OVERVIEW

The ESFj "Enthusiast" represents to me "the avid youngster" of the social world. She began life with much promise. Then again, she tends to have self-defeating behaviours and actions.

Enthusiasts can befall into places and people where they may suffer. They tend to refuse help from others in dealing with life. They can struggle with romance. They tend to choose relations that may lead to regret, let down, or even abuse.

Enthusiasts believe that the path to love and joy comes from service to others. This can hold them back from focusing on their ambitions. This selfless nature may get in the way of their happiness.

Enthusiasts shun chances for pleasure. They tend to show a reluctance to grant enjoyment. They likely remain carefree towards those who care about them. They may even reject genuinely caring partners.

Enthusiasts like to gain peace of mind by losing sight of themselves in care to others. On the other hand, they soon come to the dull thought that advancing in their career holds no importance.

Enthusiasts have strong tastes and likings. They keenly show others their likes and dislikes. They enjoy having concern for others. They tend to reflect the values of the community.

## MODEL A: THE "ESFJ" ENTHUSIAST

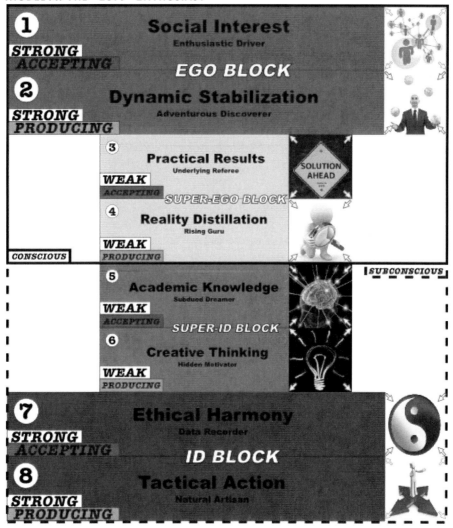

## ATTITUDE ANALYSIS: EGO BLOCK

1. ENTHUSIASTIC DRIVER - SOCIAL INTEREST (SI)
"...LIFE IS WITH PEOPLE..."

Social Interest is the rational first attitude. It leads the enthusiast to view the world regarding what roles people play. Therefore, SI is about having an extreme need to be part of the social world. She will find it most natural to care and entertain for the needs of others. This allows her to achieve her sense of duty.

Enthusiasts may fit into the role of provider. They have a need to perform acts as direct expressions of their feelings. For example, they choose to cook a meal for their partner. This action has to mean for the bond they share.

Hence, SI is a view that life is with people. It leads the enthusiast to have courteous and tactful dealings with others. They have a need to get along peacefully.

## 2. ADVENTUROUS DISCOVERER - DYNAMIC STABILIZATION (DS)
### "...TO REMAIN ANCHORED TO THE KNOWN..."

Dynamic Stabilization is the irrational second attitude. It helps produce insights that the SI mindset needs. Real world insights go through a safe make process. For example, the enthusiast puts one hundred dollars in a bank. They know that the transaction implies no other facts. They do not expect an unusual thing to happen as a result.

Enthusiasts tend to give real answers as opposed to abstract ones. In other words, they tend to be practical people. DS keeps them fixed to the concrete world. For example, they prefer to stick with social norms.

Enthusiasts are realists who live in the here and now. They tend to focus on what is, rather than what could be. DS allows them to remain anchored to the known. For example, they allow some extra time when leaving on a trip. They may do this since the world has unpredictable things that could make them late. On the other hand, very few unpredictable things could come along and make them early if they did not give themselves extra time.

Hence, DS as the second attitude serves as a kind of prompt to the SI attitude that the social world needs a level of skill to navigate it. The DS mindset allows the enthusiast to cope with a variety of stimuli in the world.

**ATTITUDE ANALYSIS: SUPER-EGO BLOCK**

### 3. UNDERLYING REFEREE - PRACTICAL RESULTS (PR)
"...TO TAKE PRACTICAL ACTION..."

Practical Results is the third rational attitude. It is one-half of the super-ego and conscience behind the stronger ego attitudes. For the enthusiast, actions leading to useful outcomes do not show on the surface much.

They tend to take practical measures behind the scenes. For example, they surprise their partner with a birthday party. They did all the planning and preparation in secret.

Enthusiasts may end up as modest small business owners. They may enjoy getting quick results. They will tend to stick to tried and tested principles. They do not get involved in unusual ways to build wealth.

As a complex, the enthusiast may become cross when plans go wrong. She expects results in the best way possible. She does not want to get involved with an unsuitable team.

Hence, PR as the third attitude leads the enthusiast to know how to get results. For example, she decides that speed dating is more useful than going out clubbing.

### 4. RISING GURU - REALITY DISTILLATION (RD)
"...TO MAKE FAULTY JUDGEMENTS..."

Reality Distillation is the fourth irrational attitude. It is the second half of the super-ego and conscience behind the stronger ego attitudes. As the producing attitude for the PR attitude, it is the weak need to see core truths. The enthusiast will avoid getting to the root of reality. She will prefer to keep her common sense intact.

As a phobic mindset, this explains why enthusiasts cannot see clearly through the extra details in the world. This can easily lead them to make faulty judgments about people. They end up with the wrong ideas some of the time. Thus, they are usually hard to please. On the other hand, this lack of seeking core truths allows them to focus on the drama of real life without concern for the details.

Hence, RD is a timid attitude for the enthusiast. It results in a lack of need to see the crux of matters. With a weak need to see through the distortions present in reality, they may miss crucial details. Also, they will not seem to comment on the world appropriately.

## ATTITUDE ANALYSIS: SUPER-ID BLOCK

### 5. SUBDUED DREAMER - ACADEMIC KNOWLEDGE (AK)
"...THE INNER NEED TO KNOW THE WORLD..."

Academic Knowledge is the fifth rational attitude. It is one-half of the super-id, the conscience of the id. For the enthusiast, this mindset is restless in appreciating how things work. The conscious attitudes have sought upon the importance of relationships. The AK attitude equates to the inner need to know the world. For example, at college, there is a naïve need to make sense of their course.

This swayable attitude may not ask for help in its special wish to know things. For example, having built their social network they may like to question their relations.

Hence, AK is a dormant attitude that wants the enthusiast to figure out the world. A person with a strong conscious AK attitude can provoke a restart of this desire.

### 6. HIDDEN MOTIVATOR - CREATIVE THINKING (CT)
"...TO NOTICE TRENDS IN REALITY..."

Creative Thinking is the sixth irrational attitude. It is the second half of the super-id, the conscience of the id. For the enthusiast, it yields results of the AK attitude by seeing potentials. This attitude does not judge reality well until helped by someone with CT as a conscious attitude.

As the hidden agenda of the enthusiast, they make like to notice trends in reality. They may need help with this weak area of their subconscious mind.

Hence, CT is the weak attitude that the world is full of possibilities. For example, the enthusiast may from time to time discuss their ideas for a better life.

**ATTITUDE ANALYSIS: ID BLOCK**

7. DATA RECORDER - ETHICAL HARMONY (EH)
"...TO DO THE RIGHT THING..."

Ethical Harmony is the seventh rational attitude. It is one-half of the id, the most instinctual self. As we delve into the core of the enthusiast's mind, we find concern for keeping harmony between self and others. The EH mindset will fulfil itself under periods of stress or upset. For example, they spot potential conflict on a night out and keep a substantial distance to avoid any discord.

Hence, EH is a strong subconscious mindset that provides the enthusiast on a whim to do the right thing. They may use their well-built moral codes to avoid quarrels with others.

8. NATURAL ARTISAN - TACTICAL ACTION (TA)
"...AN AUTOMATIC ZEST FOR LIFE..."

Tactical Action is the irrational eighth attitude. It is the second half of the id, the most instinctual self. At the core of the enthusiast's mind, we find an automatic zest for life. Any details in the world call for a down-to-earth reaction. This attitude keeps them tuned to the here and now.

Hence, TA is a strong subconscious mindset that keeps the enthusiast fixed to the world with genuine feedback. Therefore, they can enjoy what life has to offer.

**PERSONAL DEVELOPMENT FOR ESFJ'S**

Enthusiasts tend to seek out people and relations. This can make them come across as "socialites". They enjoy spending time with others. However, they do not always know when to abstain from helping others. I suggest that they focus on themselves more and tone down their need to serve.

Enthusiasts tend to patronise others. They enjoy a caring role. They do not value others prying into their life. I suggest that they become more open and allow others to assist them in personal matters. They need to start appreciating outside help as a useful thing.

Enthusiasts more often than not continue to live in the drama of their lives. They routinely get prone to reacting highly strung by events. They do not usually have a detached focus on their lives. I suggest that they learn the art of introspection to induce more focus.

FAMOUS EXAMPLES OF ESFJ'S

- Bill Clinton (42nd US President)
- Eddie Murphy (American Actor)
- Michael Palin, CBE (English Comedian)
- Geri Halliwell (British Singer-Songwriter)

## THE "ENTP" SEARCHER

### OVERVIEW

The ENTp "Searcher" represents to me "the shy extrovert" of the social world. He cannot choose which language works more efficient, Java, PHP or Klingon? He desires respect. He wants kudos. He wants success. Lastly, he wants others to hold him in high regards.

Searchers have a need to attain a spot of distinction over others. They need to express themselves. They want to intrigue others.

Searchers need love and respect from others. They take pleasure in overwhelming others with the force of their idioms. They want to mesmerise and catch the attention of others. They like a fusion between people.

Searchers tend to have a subtle "image-consciousness". They have an aversion to rejection. They prefer to observe others before making their approach. They want to unite with others. They do this via careful looking, hearing and even touching.

Searchers call others to their visions. They see much potential in the universe. They pursue new challenges to satisfy these needs. Ultimately, they want some fame. This could come from travelling the globe as a public speaker or exploring space as an astronaut.

Searchers have a cheerful nature. They take pleasure in a detached interest. They focus a lot on ideas. They have a keen sense of adventure.

## MODEL A: THE "ENTP" SEARCHER

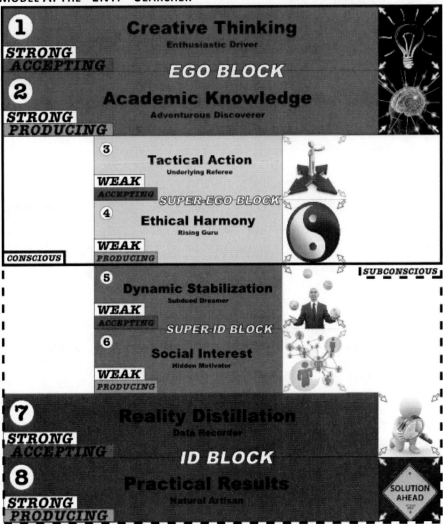

**ATTITUDE ANALYSIS: EGO BLOCK**

1. ENTHUSIASTIC DRIVER - CREATIVE THINKING (CT)
*"...ALWAYS LOOKING FOR MORE MEANINGS..."*

Creative Thinking is the irrational first attitude. It leads the searcher to live in a world of the unknown thriving with possibilities. Therefore, CT is like having a lens that reflects greater truths. He will like finding the 'big picture'.

Searchers are always looking for more meanings in things. To deal with reality, he must account for the wider scope. For example, a fossil hints at a full dinosaur, or the increase of clouds in the sky hints at a coming thunderstorm. He needs to explore the broader context. This will change his perception of the whole by understanding its parts.

The CT mindset leads the searcher to adapt to exploit growing chances. He does this to see the potential for fulfilling his visions. He does not wait to explore the unknown. For example, he aims for promotion at work often. This kind of shrewdness allows him to be very flexible.

Hence, CT is a need to welcome the unknown always. It leads the searcher to adjust to the unexpected. They have an approval of the hectic nature of the world.

### 2. ADVENTUROUS DISCOVERER - ACADEMIC KNOWLEDGE (AK)
*"...TO SEEK HOW THINGS WORK..."*

Academic Knowledge is the rational second attitude. It helps produce insights that the CT mindset needs. Social trends go through study to reveal their fundamental nature. For example, the searcher sees a trend in the social world. They aim to make sense of it by reasoning.

Searchers tend to seek how things work after making a discovery. They do not focus on growing their ideas entirely. AK assists their grasp of observable facts. For example, Albert Einstein exposed the power of the atom. It was not until others built upon his ideas did we get the A-bomb.

Searchers are futurists who live in the future. They tend to focus on what could be, rather than what is. AK allows them to build new abstract insights. For example, they follow the ethos that practice makes perfect.

Hence, AK as the second attitude serves as a prompt to the CT attitude that there is wisdom to form through the mysteries of life. The AK mindset allows the searcher to reflect on what they have seen through their intuition.

## ATTITUDE ANALYSIS: SUPER-EGO

### 3. UNDERLYING REFEREE - TACTICAL ACTION (TA)
*"...TO ACT IN RESPONSE TO THE ENVIRONMENT..."*

Tactical Action is the third irrational attitude. It is one-half of the super-ego and the conscience behind the stronger ego attitudes. For the searcher, down-to-earth reactions to the world do not show on the surface much. They tend to have no concern for the past or future. For example, they like to live in the moment at parties. They do so after a drink or two and having observed the place.

Searchers may end up as reserved partygoers. They may enjoy a situation in which they can let loose. They will tend to act in response to the environment in cool ways. They do not like to enjoy life alone.

As a complex, the searcher may become cross when others step into the way of their pleasure seeking. He expects to enjoy life with a low regard to the costs. He does not want to get involved with reclusive people.

Hence, TA as the third attitude leads the searcher to take part in the surroundings. He takes great pleasure in living an exciting life.

### 4. RISING GURU - ETHICAL HARMONY (EH)
*"...A WEAK NEED TO UPHOLD HARMONY..."*

Ethical Harmony is the fourth rational attitude. It is the conscience behind the stronger ego attitudes. As the producing attitude of the TA role attitude, it is the weak need to maintain a moral code of conduct. The searcher will avoid acting on moral judgments. He will prefer to keep his buoyant nature intact.

As a phobic mindset, this explains why searchers do not know well how to respect others. This can easily lead them to offend people. Their conduct to others is often feeble at best. Thus, they are usually hard to be acquainted with. On the other hand, this lack of good manners lets them focus on their worldly interests without fear of vexing others.

Hence, EH is a timid attitude for the searcher. It results in a kind of messy tact with others. With a weak need to uphold harmony in their relations, they may lose friends. Also, they will not seem hold grudges for too long.

## ATTITUDE ANALYSIS: SUPER-ID BLOCK

### 5. SUBDUED DREAMER - DYNAMIC STABILIZATION (DS)
"...TO FIXATE ON THE KNOWN..."

Dynamic Stabilization is the fifth irrational attitude. It is one-half of the super-id, the conscience of the id. For the searcher, this mindset is restless in anchoring them to the known. The conscious attitudes have sought upon the trends in the world. The DS attitude equates to the inner need to deal with a muddled reality. For example, at a party, there is a naïve need to obey social customs.

This swayable attitude may not ask for help in its private wish to concern them with the chaotic nature of the world. For example, after years of seeing trends, they may want to retire to a calm lifestyle.

Hence, DS is a dormant attitude that wants the searcher to fixate on the known. A person with a strong conscious DS attitude can provoke a restart of this desire.

### 6. HIDDEN MOTIVATOR - SOCIAL INTEREST (SI)
"...VALUE A LIFE WITH PEOPLE..."

Social Interest is the sixth rational attitude. It is the second half of the super-id, the conscience of the id. For the searcher, it yields results of the DS attitude by valuing relations. This attitude does not judge reality well until helped by someone with SI as a conscious attitude.

As the hidden agenda of the searcher, they may like to value a life with people more. They may need help with this weak area of their subconscious mind.

Hence, SI is the weak attitude that wants to relate socially and build a following. For example, the searcher may from time to time get a group of people together for a party.

## ATTITUDE ANALYSIS: ID BLOCK

### 7. DATA RECORDER - REALITY DISTILLATION (RD)
"...TO NEGOTIATE WITH OTHERS..."

Reality Distillation is the seventh irrational attitude. It is one-half of the id, the most instinctual self. As we delve into the core of the searcher's mind, we find concern for arguing through the extra details in reality. The RD mindset will fulfil itself under periods of stress or upset. For example, when pressured they will have a sharp tongue for cutting out the fuzz with others.

Hence, RD is a strong subconscious mindset that provides the searcher on a whim for negotiating with others. They may use this skill to stay focused and on-task.

### 8. NATURAL ARTISAN - PRACTICAL RESULTS (PR)
"...AN AUTOMATIC ZEST FOR BUSINESS LOGIC..."

Practical Results is the eighth rational attitude. It is the second half of the id, the most instinctual self. At the core of the searcher's mind, we find an automatic zest for business logic. Any goals in the world call for a practical system. This attitude keeps them tuned to the skill for finding the best ways to achieve a plan.

Hence, PR is a strong subconscious mindset that keeps the searcher on the lookout for results. Therefore, they can make excellent additions to a corporate team.

## PERSONAL DEVELOPMENT FOR ENTP'S

Searchers tend to seek out people to build a following. This can make them come across as self-centred. They enjoy having others do what they say. However, they do not always find the right emotional legroom from people. I suggest that they deal with their self-approval needs and learn how to become more tactful.

Searchers tend to do very well in education. They are often high achievers. They do not like to fail. They are prone to exhausting others for their gain. I suggest that they build their social network to find like-minded people to help with their goals.

Searchers more often than not have a needy nature. They are prone to rounding up others when they need results. They do not always spend the time to work things out on their own. I suggest that they learn the art of introspection to solve their problems more.

### FAMOUS EXAMPLES OF ENTP'S
- Albert Einstein (Theoretical Physicist)
- Aushra Augusta (Lithuanian Psychologist)
- Ayn Rand (Russian-American Novelist)
- Sigmund Freud (Austrian Psychiatrist)

## THE "ISFP" MEDIATOR

### OVERVIEW

The ISFp "Mediator" represents to me "the outgoing introvert" of the social world. He displays constant patterns of distinct cyclic changes in mood. His conduct can change from one day to the next. He has erratic energy levels.

Mediators vary in the midst of hope and fear. They have phases of sharp vision. However, they also have periods of confusion and boredom.

Mediators have a need to seek out people in a pushy way. However, they also like time spent on their own. They tend to work as a means to play harder. They often shift their line of work.

Mediators will react with heated outbursts when stirred up the wrong way. They will most likely alienate you during this time. However, after they find their calm again, they will act as though nothing happened.

Mediators have a warm nature. They have a need for comfort. They often greet others with a gentle smile.

## MODEL A: THE "ISFP" MEDIATOR

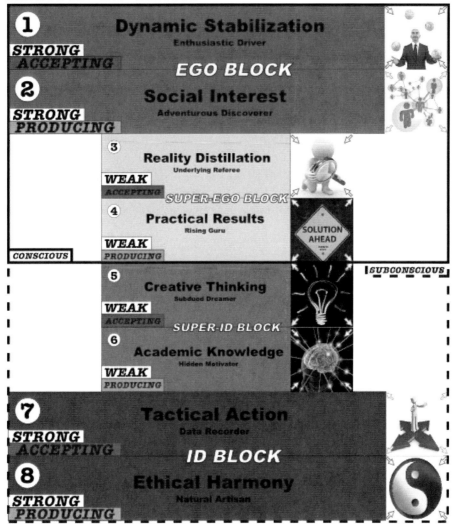

### ATTITUDE ANALYSIS: EGO BLOCK

1. ENTHUSIASTIC DRIVER - DYNAMIC STABILIZATION (DS)
"...TO CREATE ORDER OUT OF THE CHAOS OF LIFE..."

Dynamic Stabilization is the irrational first attitude. It leads the mediator to live in a world of always changing stimuli. Therefore, DS is like having a stabiliser system that deals with reality. He will even out reality and give it a consistent meaning for himself.

Mediators would not believe for a moment that the world is logical. To deal with the mess, in reality, they must scan the environment and give it some sense. For example, they need to attend a meeting and decide to leave early as to avoid things that could make them late. They need to keep anchored to the known. This will keep them at ease.

The DS mindset leads the mediator to adapt to clutter in an untidy reality. He does this to live in harmony with nature. He does not like unexpected events. For example, he loses his job and abhors the thought of claiming dole money. This kind of alertness allows him to take action to avoid such things in the future.

Hence, DS is a need to create order out of the chaos of life. It leads the mediator to find one's feet in the world. They have a need to live a stress-free life with great peace of mind.

## 2. ADVENTUROUS DISCOVERER - SOCIAL INTEREST (SI)
### "...QUITE THE SOCIABLE INTROVERT..."

Social Interest is the rational second attitude. It helps produce insights that the DS mindset needs. Common sense combines with an acceptance of the roles people play. For example, the mediator learns to treat people fairly. They know how to obey the norms of politeness. They do not expect people to disrupt the harmony of a situation.

Mediators tend to seek out people. In other words, they tend to be somewhat outgoing. SI keeps them attentive to the social world. For example, they may like to attend parties often.

Mediators are optimists who live in the here and now. They tend to focus on the present with a sanguine view of the future. SI allows them to perform acts as a direct display of their feelings. For example, they like to collaborate with others on projects. This action has meaning for them.

Hence, SI as the second attitude serves as a kind of prompt to the DS attitude that the social world has many relations to form in it. The SI mindset allows the mediator to look for new relationships.

## ATTITUDE ANALYSIS: SUPER-EGO BLOCK

### 3. UNDERLYING REFEREE - REALITY DISTILLATION (RD)
"...TO DISCERN REALITY WITHOUT ANY FLUFF..."

Reality Distillation is the third irrational attitude. It is one-half of the super-ego and conscience behind the stronger ego attitudes. For the mediator, seeking core truths does not show on the surface much. They tend to get to the root of reality behind the scenes. For example, they use negotiation skills when closing a deal. They do well in sales.

Mediators may end up as modest salespeople. They may enjoy getting to the source of objections from others. They will tend to do so in reserved ways. They do not know when to drop a debate when others have apparently given their doubts.

As a complex, the mediator may become cross when they cannot make out truths. He expects to grasp reality in a painless way. He likes to know what went wrong in his need to understand others.

Hence, RD as the third attitude leads the mediator to discern reality without any fluff. For example, he has to sell an idea to someone and tries to keep things as real as possible.

### 4. RISING GURU - PRACTICAL RESULTS (PR)
"...CANNOT TURN IDEAS INTO REALITY EASILY..."

Practical Results is the fourth rational attitude. It is the second half of the super-ego and conscience behind the stronger ego attitudes. As the producing attitude of the RD attitude, it is the weak need for serious results. The mediator will avoid the use of business logic. He will prefer to keep his common sense intact.

As a phobic mindset, this explains why mediators cannot turn ideas into reality quickly. This can lead them to start failed businesses. They end up with poor results. Thus, they are usually left frustrated at not having a good system to break out of their existing job. On the other hand, this lack of obtaining results allows them to focus on their melee with life without concern for building real wealth.

Hence, PR is a timid attitude for the mediator. It results in a lack of expertise in the use of business logic. With a weak skill in turning ideas into reality, they may miss the potential for building wealth. Also, they will remain somewhat content as a worker and not as an entrepreneur.

## ATTITUDE ANALYSIS: SUPER-ID BLOCK

### 5. SUBDUED DREAMER - CREATIVE THINKING (CT)
*"...TO SEE THE 'BIG PICTURE'..."*

Creative Thinking is the fifth irrational attitude. It is one-half of the super-id, the conscience of the id. For the mediator, this mindset is restless in seeing the trends in the world. The conscious attitudes have sought upon making sense of the world. The CT attitude equates to the inner need to see the 'big picture'. For example, at work, there is a naïve need to see how a system in use helps get things done.

This swayable attitude may not ask for help in its wish to see reality in a broad context. For example, after years of dealing with a chaotic world, they may prefer to think more laterally.

Hence, CT is a dormant attitude that wants the mediator to wonder what could be. A person with a strong conscious CT attitude can provoke a restart of this desire.

### 6. HIDDEN MOTIVATOR - ACADEMIC KNOWLEDGE (AK)
*"...TO UNDERSTAND ANY SUBJECT OF INTEREST..."*

Academic Knowledge is the sixth rational attitude. It is the second half of the super-id, the conscience of the id. For the mediator, it yields results of the CT attitude by valuing how things work. This attitude does not judge reality well until helped by someone with AK as a conscious attitude.

As the hidden agenda of the mediator, they may like to study the world more. They may need help with this weak area of their subconscious mind.

Hence, AK is the weak attitude that wants to understand any subject of interest. For example, the mediator may from time to time go through a period of reflection to understand a new process.

### ATTITUDE ANALYSIS: ID BLOCK

#### 7. DATA RECORDER - TACTICAL ACTION (TA)
*"...A NO-NONSENSE RESPONSE TO THE WORLD..."*

Tactical Action is the seventh irrational attitude. It is one-half of the id, the most instinctual self. As we delve into the core of the mediator's mind, we find concern for a no-nonsense response to the world. The TA mindset will fulfil itself under periods of stress or upset. For example, if they lose their job they may boldly seek out new employment right away.

Hence, TA is a strong subconscious mindset that provides the mediator on a whim to take action. They may use this skill to keep their lives moving forward.

#### 8. NATURAL ARTISAN - ETHICAL HARMONY (EH)
*"...AN AUTOMATIC ZEST FOR SOCIAL HARMONY."*

Ethical Harmony is the eighth rational attitude. It is the second half of the id, the most instinctual self. At the core of the mediator's mind, we find an automatic zest for social harmony. Any discord in the world calls for harmonisation. This attitude keeps them tuned the skill for using tact to maintain agreements between people.

Hence, EH is a strong subconscious mindset that keeps the mediator on the lookout for friction. Therefore, they can make good referees in team games.

## PERSONAL DEVELOPMENT FOR ISFP'S

Mediators tend to have an erratic conduct towards others. This can make them come across as unstable. They are prone to anxiety. I suggest that they deal with their sensitive nature by learning how to become more objective.

Mediators tend to have an outgoing nature. This can make them seem more like an extrovert. They enjoy spending time with others. However, they do not always like the company of others. I suggest they deal with their ambivert nature by finding the right balance between seeking out people and focusing on their needs.

Mediators more often than not live in the here and now. They are prone to instinctually react to the world as-is. They do not always have realistic expectations. I suggest that they use planning and appreciate the reality of an ever-changing world.

### FAMOUS EXAMPLES OF ISFP'S

- Sarah Chalke (Canadian-American Actress)
- John Candy (Canadian Comedian)
- Ozzy Osbourne (English Singer-Songwriter)
- Matt LeBlanc (American Actor)

# THE BETA QUADRA

Summary:
- Intellectual Age: adolescent/teenage
- Group Mantra: constant and never-ending accomplishment
- Stimulus: artistic expression of romantic and abstract ideas
- Typical behaviour: theatrical, generous, rowdy
- Social Role: catalysts/Renaissance actors/introducing new orders and organisation for the resistance of the environment
- Political philosophy: weak individualism/confederation of individuals
- Epistemology: agnosticism/pragmatism/practical knowledge
- Moral dilemma: Can we strive to reform an old and divided society to revive and unite?

Members:
- The "ISTj" Inspector
- The "ENFj" Actor
- The "ESTp" Marshal
- The "INFp" Romantic

A combination of ST's and NF's which translates to "Rebel Pragmatists" and "Revivalist Humanists" whom together form, in a nutshell, society's Practicality & Spirituality division. The kind of people who want to grow us spiritually in a practical matter of fact way for the rest of the Socion.

## THE "ISTJ" INSPECTOR

### OVERVIEW

The ISTj "Inspector" represents to me "the mysterious recluse" of the social world. He can live out his days quite happily on his own in a neatly arranged home with the occasional visits from friends.

Inspectors have an out of the ordinary challenge. They have excellent people skills. On the other hand, they prefer isolation. They tend to show a superficial charm towards others to mask their introverted nature.

Inspectors may struggle with anger management issues. They can strike back against any perceived slights. They love nothing more than to stand their ground with people that have provoked them in some way.

Inspectors may end up spiritual with a quest to rid the world of evildoers. In due course, they blossom into men entering the social scene more.

They will attend parties with women in tow. They do display a firm restraint and no-nonsense stance.

Inspectors like behaving steadfast and firm. They usually stand their ground with people and situations. They remain disciplined, cautious, and practical most of the time.

## MODEL A: THE "ISTJ" INSPECTOR

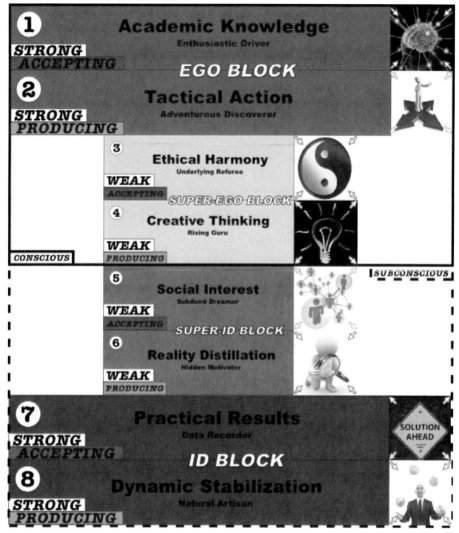

## ATTITUDE ANALYSIS: EGO BLOCK

1. ENTHUSIASTIC DRIVER - ACADEMIC KNOWLEDGE (AK)
"...REALISTIC UNDERSTANDING..."

Academic Knowledge is the rational first attitude. It leads the inspector to make sense of reality through structural logic. Therefore, AK is like a guidebook used to make sense of real-world problems. He will refer to his private library a lot when dealing with reality.

Inspectors are always adding new facts to their in-house guidebooks. To deal with anything he may have to look up his 'how to' guide on the subject. He only requires a surface understanding of things to work them.

The AK mindset leads the inspector to need a sound knowledge of whatever takes his interest. He does, however, prefer to know things in a matter-of-fact way. He does not need in-depth theoretical answers.

Hence, AK is a low-bandwidth or realistic understanding of the world. It leads the inspector to know just enough of something to operate it well.

## 2. ADVENTUROUS DISCOVERER - TACTICAL ACTION (TA)
### "...STRAIGHTFORWARD PERCEPTIONS..."

Tactical Action is the irrational second attitude. It helps produce insights that the AK mindset needs. Theories and ideas go through a practical filter. For example, the inspector wants to build his or her computer. They may decide to follow a 'how to' guide strictly and not deviate from the instructions.

Inspectors learn best through lessons. In other words, they need a bottom-up approach to learning. TA allows them to produce practical insights. For example, they choose to share a quote with others that have a very pragmatic way of looking at things. In most cases, this style of learning results in a slower albeit firm grasp of something.

Inspectors enjoy their spare time in conventional ways. They are realists who live in the here and now. They are not usually idealists. They tend to focus on the empirical not the speculative.

Hence, TA as the second attitude serves as a kind of prompt to the AK attitude that the world requires straightforward perceptions. The TA attitude allows the inspector to gather facts to know the world.

**ATTITUDE ANALYSIS: SUPER-EGO BLOCK**

### 3. UNDERLYING REFEREE - ETHICAL HARMONY (EH)
"...A MORAL CONSCIENCE..."

Ethical Harmony is the third rational attitude. It is one-half of the super-ego and conscience behind the stronger ego attitudes. For the inspector, inner feelings do not appear on the surface much.

Inspectors may end up needing to make an honest living. They like to treat others how they would expect others to treat them.

As a complex, the inspector may become cross when his ethics are threatened. He expects others to accept this strong grasp of reality. He does not tolerate treacherous behaviour in others. He will usually do the right thing when dealing with conflict.

Hence, EH as the third attitude leads the inspector to have a moral conscience. For example, this provides them with a real sense of justice.

### 4. RISING GURU - CREATIVE THINKING (CT)
"...AVOID MAKING ASSOCIATIONS..."

Creative Thinking is the fourth irrational attitude. It is the conscience behind the stronger ego attitudes. As the producing attitude for the EH role attitude, it is a weak need to see the 'big picture'. The inspector will avoid making associations between things in the world. He will prefer to keep his short-range knowledge intact.

As a phobic mindset, this explains why inspectors cannot project well into the future. This can easily lead him to focus on the world as-is. They end up concerned with the facts and details. Thus, they are usually pragmatists and not prophets. On the other hand, this avoidance of the 'big picture' allows them to focus on the here and now.

Hence, CT is a timid attitude for the inspector. It results in a lack of need to forecast the future. With a weak need to see broad contexts, they may miss chances for progress. Also, they will rarely question things that have global reaches.

## ATTITUDE ANALYSIS: SUPER-ID BLOCK

### 5. SUBDUED DREAMER - SOCIAL INTEREST (SI)
"...THE INNER NEED TO RELATE TO OTHERS..."

Social Interest is the fifth rational attitude. It is one-half of the super-id, the conscience of the id. For the inspector, this mindset is restless in appreciating the role we all play. The conscious attitudes have sought to know the world in a matter-of-fact way. The SI attitude equates to the inner need to relate to others. For example, at a social event, there is a naïve need to engage with others in conversation.

This swayable attitude may not ask for help in its private wish to get on with others. For example, a handshake as a way of accepting the roles between people who are friends without literally broadcasting it.

Hence, SI is a dormant attitude that wants the inspector to associate more with others. An individual with a strong conscious SI attitude can provoke a restart of this desire.

### 6. HIDDEN MOTIVATOR - REALITY DISTILLATION (RD)
"...TO KNOW REALITY WITHOUT ANY FLUFF..."

Reality Distillation is the sixth irrational attitude. It is the second half of the super-id, the conscience of the id. For the inspector, it yields results of the SI attitude by appreciating core truths. This attitude does not judge reality well until helped by someone with RD as a conscious attitude.

As the hidden agenda of the inspector, they may like to know reality without any fluff. They may need help with this weak area of their subconscious mind.

Hence, RD is the weak attitude that the world has more going on that what is visible on the surface. For example, the inspector may claim to have clairvoyant powers.

**ATTITUDE ANALYSIS: ID BLOCK**

### 7. DATA RECORDER - PRACTICAL RESULTS (PR)
"...TO DO SOMETHING PRACTICAL..."

Practical Results is the seventh rational attitude. It is one-half of the id, the most instinctual self. As we delve into the core of the inspector's mind, we find concern for decisive thoughts. The PR mindset will fulfil itself under periods of stress or upset. For example, they face losing their job and decide to work harder to gain a promotion.

Hence, PR is a strong subconscious mindset that provides the inspector on a whim to do something practical. They may become an entrepreneur with the right kind of support.

### 8. NATURAL ARTISAN - DYNAMIC STABILIZATION (DS)
"...AN AUTOMATIC ZEST FOR PRAGMATISM..."

Dynamic Stabilization is the irrational eighth attitude. It is the second half of the id, the most instinctual self. At the core of the inspector's mind, we find an automatic zest for pragmatism. Any aspects of reality that seem jumbled will go through a safe make process. This attitude keeps them fixed to the tried and tested.

Hence, DS is a strong subconscious mindset that keeps the inspector firmly attached to the here-and-now. Therefore, they keep a watchful eye over reality for any potential chaos.

## PERSONAL DEVELOPMENT FOR ISTJ'S

Inspectors tend to get depressed easily since they live in the here and now. This can make them seem by far vulnerable to sadness. They may live a life prone to anxiety. I suggest that they deal with their weak planning skills by enlisting the help of yearly planners and goal setting.

Inspectors can start new ventures. However, they more often than not get stuck to push them beyond a small-scale business. I suggest that they team up with people who have a knack for long-range planning to advance their growing enterprise to the next level.

Inspectors can quickly judge others based on first impressions. They can change their opinion over time albeit in slow and uneven ways. They do not always react well to others who act foolishly towards them. I suggest that they learn to embrace their weak skill to get to the root of reality concerning a person to make sound judgements.

### FAMOUS EXAMPLES OF ISTJ'S

- Dr Phil (American Television Personality)
- Anthony Hopkins, CBE (Welsh Actor)
- Kirsty Young (Scottish TV Presenter)
- Catherine Zeta-Jones (Welsh Actress)
- Gordon Ramsay (British Television Personality)

# The "ENFj" Actor

## Overview

The ENFj "Actor" represents to me "the Jedi Master" of the social world. She will use The Force as her ally and Darth Vader and the Emperor. Her innate grasp of social dynamics gives her great powers to sway others to act. The essential gift of this type equates to their ability to empower and encourage others.

Actors display a show of neatness and care. They act as though having come from royalty demanding high standards and respect from others. They hate disorder. They can feel overwhelmed by the array of things that need doing.

Actors are avid transformers of culture. They will work relentlessly to bring about change in how people currently think about things. For example, they will reform mindsets towards something that is now all the rage.

Actors repeatedly have a conduct similar to that described in Obsessive-compulsive personality disorder (OCPD). They love nothing more than to keeping busy, working, maintaining efficiency and success. Any flaws, defects or mistakes in their work or plans they find intolerable.

Actors are the backbones of any organisation or family unit. They are conscientious types who flourish within cultures such as ours in which the work ethic thrives. They will not rest until a job achieves a high level of satisfaction.

Actors tend to behave in a histrionic way. They also have an overt control of themselves. They mostly show firm emotions and concern in situations.

## MODEL A: THE "ENFJ" ACTOR

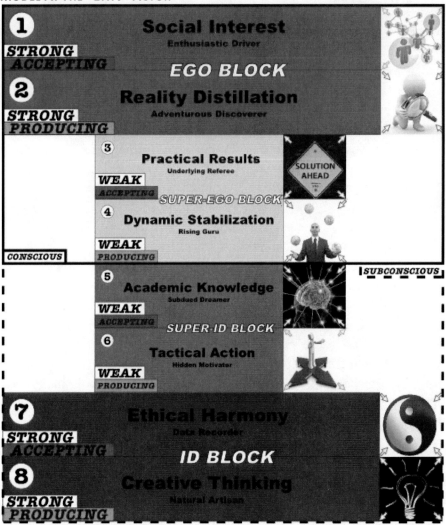

**ATTITUDE ANALYSIS: EGO BLOCK**

1. ENTHUSIASTIC DRIVER - SOCIAL INTEREST (SI)
"...LIFE IS WITH PEOPLE..."

Social Interest is the rational first attitude. It leads the actor to view the world regarding what roles people play. Therefore, SI is about having an extreme need to be part of the social world. She will find it most natural to care and entertain for the needs of others. This allows her to achieve her sense of duty.

Actors may fit into the role of motivator. They have a need to inspire others to direct action. For example, they host a keynote speech on the latest innovations. This presentation aims to sway others to join their cult for the item they are introducing.

Hence, SI is a view that life is with people. It leads the actor to have courteous and tactful dealings with others. They have a need to get along peacefully.

### 2. ADVENTUROUS DISCOVERER - REALITY DISTILLATION (RD)
*"...REDUCING THE FLUFF..."*

Reality Distillation is the irrational second attitude. It helps produce insights that the SI mindset needs. Real world insights go through a refining process. For example, the actor shows concern for their friends. They want to know the core truth of their relationship. They do not expect others to deceive them about the matter.

Actors have a keen eye for reducing the fluff in the social world. In other words, they tend to want to get to the root of reality. RD keeps them on guard against the extra details in the world. For example, they may observe a man and woman as best friends and use probing questions that should uncover just how they feel about each other.

Hence, RD as the second attitude serves as a kind of prompt to the SI attitude that the social world needs revealing to steer it. The RD mindset allows the actor to query a range of people and situations to unveil the truth.

### ATTITUDE ANALYSIS: SUPER EGO BLOCK

### 3. UNDERLYING REFEREE - PRACTICAL RESULTS (PR)
*"...TO TAKE PRACTICAL ACTION..."*

Practical Results is the third rational attitude. It is one-half of the super-ego and conscience behind the stronger ego attitudes. For the actor, actions leading to useful outcomes do not show on the surface much. They tend to take practical measures behind the scenes. For example, they chair a meeting for a future event. They do all the red tape and budgeting in secret.

Actors may end up as modest small business owners. They may enjoy getting shrewd results. They will tend to try out new ideas and concepts. They like to take risks that involve swaying others to buy their services or goods.

As a complex, the actor may become cross when plans go wrong. She expects results in the best way possible. She does not want to get involved with a weak team.

Hence, PR as the third attitude leads the actor to know how to get results. For example, she decides that a romantic meal makes the ideal date.

### 4. Rising Guru - Dynamic Stabilization (DS)
*"...LACK OF STABILISING REALITY..."*

Dynamic Stabilization is the fourth irrational attitude. It is the second half of the super-ego and conscience behind the stronger ego attitudes. As the producing attitude for the PR attitude, it is a weak need to anchor to the known. The actor will avoid being a realist. She will prefer to keep her idealisms intact.

As a phobic mindset, this explains why actors cannot stick to the tried and tested. This can easily lead them to explore idealist views of the world. They do not care too much about first impressions. Thus, they are usually fair in their dealings with others. On the other hand, this lack of stabilising reality allows them to focus on the drama of real life without being too judgmental.

Hence, DS is a timid attitude for the actor. It results in a seldom need to accept reality as-is. With a weak need to make reality have a consistent meaning for them, they may miss precise details. Also, they will not seem to live in the here and now.

## ATTITUDE ANALYSIS: SUPER ID BLOCK

### 5. SUBDUED DREAMER - ACADEMIC KNOWLEDGE (AK)
*"...THE INNER NEED TO KNOW THE WORLD..."*

Academic Knowledge is the fifth rational attitude. It is one-half of the super-id, the conscience of the id. For the actor, this mindset is restless in appreciating how things work. The conscious attitudes have sought upon the importance of relationships. The AK attitude equates to the inner need to know the world. For example, in business, there is a naïve need to make sense of the accounts.

This swayable attitude may not ask for help in its private wish to know a thing. For example, having built their social network they may like to question their relations.

Hence, AK is a dormant attitude that wants the actor to figure out the world. A person with a strong conscious AK attitude can provoke a restart of this desire.

### 6. HIDDEN MOTIVATOR - TACTICAL ACTION (TA)
*"...TO LIVE IN THE HERE AND NOW..."*

Tactical Action is the sixth irrational attitude. It is the second half of the super-id, the conscience of the id. For the actor, it yields results of the AK attitude by making serious reactions to the world. This attitude does not judge reality well until helped by someone with TA as a conscious attitude.

As the hidden agenda of the actor, they may try to live in the here and now. They may need help with this weak area of their subconscious mind.

Hence, TA is the weak attitude that the world requires a sensible response. For example, the actor may from time to time get things done without concern for the past or future.

## ATTITUDE ANALYSIS: ID BLOCK

### 7. DATA RECORDER - ETHICAL HARMONY (EH)
*"...TO DO THE RIGHT THING..."*

Ethical Harmony is the seventh rational attitude. It is one-half of the id, the most instinctual self. As we delve into the core of the actor's mind, we find concern for keeping harmony between self and others. The EH mindset will fulfil itself under periods of stress or upset. For example, they may express their moral code in a hostile situation by voting with their feet and retreating.

Hence, EH is a strong subconscious mindset that provides the actor on a whim to do the right thing. They may use their well-built principles to avoid quarrels with others.

### 8. NATURAL ARTISAN - CREATIVE THINKING (CT)
*"...AN AUTOMATIC ZEST FOR IDEALISTIC OPPORTUNITIES."*

Creative Thinking is the irrational eighth attitude. It is the second half of the id, the most instinctual self. At the core of the actor's mind, we find an automatic zest for idealistic opportunities. Any chaos, in reality, they will perceive as normal. This attitude keeps them tuned to the broader contexts.

Hence, CT is a strong subconscious mindset that keeps the actor open to a world of possibilities. Therefore, they can enjoy seeing trends that others miss.

**PERSONAL DEVELOPMENT FOR ENFJ'S**

Actors tend to make great cult leaders. This can make them come across as "out of the ordinary". They enjoy heading movements and causes. However, they do not always know when to abstain from swaying others. I suggest that they focus on the here and now and value the tried and tested.

Actors tend to resemble optimists. They enjoy inspiring others into action. They do not value others prying into their lives. I suggest that they become more like realists. They need to start appreciating the fact that not everyone likes change.

Actors more often than not continue to live in the drama of their lives. They remain prone to reacting highly strung by events. They do not have a detached focus on their lives. I suggest that they learn the art of introspection to induce more focus.

FAMOUS EXAMPLES OF ENFJ'S

- Barack Obama (44th US President)
- Steve Jobs (American Businessman)
- Bono (Irish Singer)
- Heather Graham (American Actress)
- Adolf Hitler (German Politician)

## The "INFp" Romantic

### Overview

The INFp "Romantic" represents to me "the lavish loafer" of the social world. He lives a life of middle-class laziness. However, not necessarily a bad thing since he tends to have an altruistic nature. He puts the needs of society before his own.

Romantics with a home are still, in theory, homeless. They will happily live in chaos. They are not the world's tidiest people. They like indulging in fantasy on a daily basis. They also like reading comic books, telling bedtime stories and sharing their latest riddles.

Romantics are often late for meetings. They are usually well versed in something. They have an eclectic taste in music. They probably have a Michael Jackson songs of the 80s album on cassette tape. They like to collect things especially rubbish usually kept in their car.

Romantics often go unshaven. They probably have some old food in their fridge moulding away. In fact, they probably invented strong, mature cheddar for its distinct flavour. Their relationship with time is such that deadlines are rarely absolute.

Romantics make excellent social workers though dread the red tape that goes with it. They provide a noble service to society. They may benefit from sleeping regularly on a bed of nails. This will remind them that life is not easy enough to remain so calm.

Romantics often act dreamy. They like to entertain others. They engross themselves by people's inner life. They mostly have a calm manner.

## MODEL A: THE "INFP" ROMANTIC

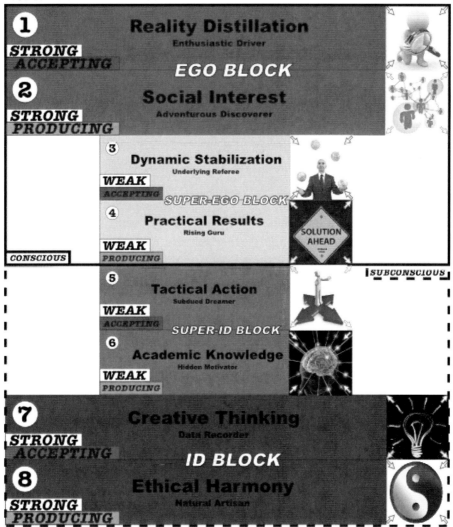

### ATTITUDE ANALYSIS: EGO BLOCK

1. ENTHUSIASTIC DRIVER - REALITY DISTILLATION (RD)
"...TO WEED THROUGH THE EXTRA DETAILS..."

Reality Distillation is the irrational first attitude. It leads the romantic to see through the distortion present, in reality, to see core truths. RD is a way for the romantic to bypass extra details. He has a gift for getting to the crux of things. He remains cynical about the truth those interpretations.

Romantics have the knack to see all the way down to fundamental reality. This allows them to weed through the extra details. Also, RD can make them seem blasé by the physical appearances of others. They merely note the likely interpretation as no less a part of the environment.

Hence, RD as the first mindset of the romantic allows him to get to the root truths. He knows how to strip things down to their essence.

### 2. ADVENTUROUS DISCOVERER - SOCIAL INTEREST (SI)
"...BUILDING DEEP RELATIONSHIPS WITH PEOPLE..."

Social Interest is the rational second attitude. It yields results of the RD mindset by giving the romantic the skill to accept the roles people play. He can be quite sociable as a result. He is renowned for building deep relationships with people. He constantly wants to know the real you. With no trouble, they see a person for who they are without getting distracted by extra details.

Romantics are usually humanists with a concern for the wellbeing of others. They will prefer to accept the depth of spirit in others. They seldom surprise themselves by the shallow details in the world.

Hence, SI as the second mindset of the romantic lets them form long-lasting relationships with others. They know how to get to know a person deeply.

**ATTITUDE ANALYSIS: SUPER-EGO BLOCK**

### 3. UNDERLYING REFEREE - DYNAMIC STABILIZATION (DS)
"...TO STABILISE THEIR PERCEPTIONS OF REALITY..."

Dynamic Stabilization is the third irrational attitude. It is one-half of the super-ego and conscience behind the stronger ego attitudes. DS lets the romantic anchor to the tried and tested. They may deal with people based on first impressions. They prefer to stabilise their perceptions of reality to the known.

Romantics have a weak need to make sense of reality. They enjoy a sense of routine in life. Also, their calm demeanour in most situations is the result of obeying social norms.

Hence, DS as the third mindset defines the man behind the mask. The romantic has a need for a steady way to provide humanistic values to the world. Therefore, it suits them to have a personal mission to do so, backed by the stability of routine.

### 4. RISING GURU - PRACTICAL RESULTS (PR)
"...A WEAK SKILL TO TURN IDEAS INTO REALITY..."

Practical Results is the fourth rational attitude. It is the second half of the super-ego and conscience behind the stronger ego attitudes. As the producing mindset for the DS attitude, it is the weak need to get results. The romantic has a soft skill to turn ideas into reality.

As a phobic mindset, this explains why romantics tend to sway towards mysticism. They do not know well how to create a system out of their ideas. On the other hand, they do not worry themselves with building wealth as they are usually busy doing a noble service to society.

Hence, PR is the timid mindset of the romantic that does not want to get involved in business ventures. They will view life as complicated enough and so will avoid it.

### ATTITUDE ANALYSIS: SUPER-ID BLOCK

### 5. SUBDUED DREAMER - TACTICAL ACTION (TA)
"...THE INNER NEED FOR SEEING REALITY AT FACE VALUE..."

Tactical Action is the fifth irrational attitude. It is one-half of the super-id, the conscience of the id. For the romantic, this mindset is restless in the use of sensible reactions. The conscious attitudes have sought social relations with core truths. The TA attitude equates to the inner need for seeing reality at face value. This swayable attitude may not ask for help in how to act more proactive.

Hence, TA is a dormant attitude that wants to accept reality as-is. A person with a strong conscious TA attitude can provoke a restart of this desire.

## 6. HIDDEN MOTIVATOR - ACADEMIC KNOWLEDGE (AK)
### "...TO KNOW THE WORLD..."

Academic Knowledge is the sixth rational attitude. It is the second half of the super-id, the conscience of the id. For the romantic, it yields results of the TA attitude by seeking to know the world. This attitude does not judge reality well until helped by someone with AK as a conscious attitude.

As the hidden agenda of the romantic, they may need help in understanding the social world. This will bridge the gap with getting to know people. They may need help with this weak area of their subconscious mind.

Hence, AK is the weak attitude that wants to have a grasp of the world. For example, the romantic needs to understand the world as a way of forming those deep relationships.

**ATTITUDE ANALYSIS: ID BLOCK**

## 7. DATA RECORDER - CREATIVE THINKING (CT)
### "...A NEED FOR TREND FORECASTING..."

Creative Thinking is the seventh irrational attitude. It is one-half of the id, the most instinctual self. As we delve into the core of the romantic's mind, we find a need for trend forecasting. The CT mindset will fulfil itself under periods of stress or upset. For example, they may begin to notice things about reality when tipsy.

Hence, CT is the strong subconscious mindset that provides the romantic with the whim to notice the 'big picture'. Over time, they will and store many bright ideas.

## 8. Natural Artisan - Ethical Harmony (EH)
### "...an automatic zest for morality..."

Ethical Harmony is the eighth rational attitude. It is the second half of the id, the most instinctual self. At the core of the romantic's mind, we find an automatic zest for morality. He may do the right thing in any given situation. For example, he backs away from a hostile situation to maintain harmony.

Hence, EH is the strong subconscious mindset that provides the romantic with a firm grip on his moral principles. This fuels his often-unruffled nature. He does not find it difficult to deal with intense situations.

### Personal development for INFp's

Romantics tend to have a weak understanding of the world. They do not live in the world of theory. They tend to create pseudo-sciences. I suggest that they get a scientific rationale of their sophisticated models.

Romantics have a weak skill to turn ideas into reality. This leads them to remain content with the sanctity of routine. I suggest that they learn about business concepts.

Romantics have a weak skill in knowing reality as-is. They concern themselves by core truths. They do not value visible reactions to the world. I suggest they learn to take things more at face value.

### Famous examples of INFp's
- Isabel Briggs Myers (American Psychological Theorist)
- Adam Sandler (American Comedian)
- Gillian Anderson (American Actress)

## The "ESTp" Marshal

### Overview

The ESTp "Marshal" represents to me "the proud coercer" of the social world. He always makes his presence known to others with his outlandish entrance or latest hairstyle. His bittersweet pilgrimage around town gets him noticed. There is hardly a day that goes by where he has not drawn attention to himself.

Marshals are practical realists. They make ideal sales consultants. They will schmooze with anyone and everyone to satisfy their need for love and respect.

Marshals come from a long line of "prince charmings". They tend to have vast amounts of experience flirting with the opposite sex.

Marshals dress in the style of the Casanova. In the workplace, they like to look good. They use their fashion style to hypnotise and control others on their way up the corporate ladder.

Marshals use fear and terror to conquer people and achieve results. They are always ready for battle. They love nothing better than to engage with others.

Marshals like behaving forceful and trying with others. They also have a creative side. They do not easily get scared. They remain for the most part tactical in their dealings with the world.

## MODEL A: THE "ESTP" MARSHAL

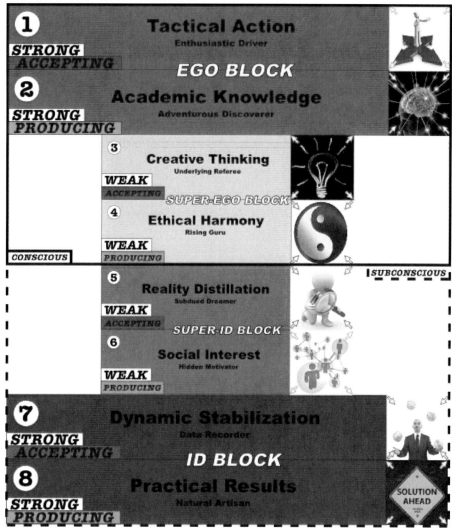

## ATTITUDE ANALYSIS: EGO BLOCK

### 1. ENTHUSIASTIC DRIVER - TACTICAL ACTION (TA)
"...RESPOND NOW TO WHAT IS HAPPENING NOW..."

Tactical Action is the irrational first attitude. It leads the marshal to call forth an obvious and natural response to the world. It has nothing to do with the way he needs to respond in any other moment. The meaning of everything is readily clear – at the time that it appears. Whatever stands out and gets his attention here-and-now is precisely what needs his attention here-and-now. His instincts at each moment will tell him what to do; there is no point in anticipating.

Marshals do not think. They do not reflect. They just react. If they feel disgusted by something, they back off from it. If they like something, they dive into it. They completely trust their immediate, instinctive response.

Hence, TA as the first mindset of the marshal lets them live life without much deliberation. For example, they will respond now to what is happening now since what happens later they will deal with later. Also, what has occurred in the past is irrelevant.

## 2. ADVENTUROUS DISCOVERER - ACADEMIC KNOWLEDGE (AK)
"...TO KNOW ENOUGH OF REALITY..."

Academic Knowledge is the rational second attitude. It yields results of the TA attitude by seeking to understand the world. The marshal uses logic to know enough of reality to come back and deal with problems later. They are go-getters not deep thinkers. For example, in social settings they can be very bold making contact with whoever takes their interest.

Hence, AK as the second mindset of the marshal provides the drive to learn from their mistakes. For example, they are willing to reflect on their experiences often in their dealings with others.

## ATTITUDE ANALYSIS: SUPER-EGO BLOCK

## 3. UNDERLYING REFEREE - CREATIVE THINKING (CT)
"...A DIRECTIVE TO SEEK OUT NEW OPPORTUNITIES..."

Creative Thinking is the third irrational attitude. It is one-half of the super-ego and conscience behind the stronger ego attitudes. CT is a way for the marshal to scan the potential here in the unknown. For example, they are more often than not dedicated people who do not stick around while others delay.

Marshals have a weak need to see the 'big picture'. They may have many ideas to make them better at achieving their goals. They make good tacticians. They are ready to dismiss failed ideas in favour of new ones.

Hence, CT as the third mindset defines the man behind the mask. The marshal has a directive to seek out new opportunities. Therefore, it suits them to take on many challenges.

### 4. RISING GURU - ETHICAL HARMONY (EH)
"...THE POTENTIAL TO OFFEND..."

Ethical Harmony is the fourth rational attitude. It is the second half of the super-ego and conscience behind the stronger ego attitudes. As the producing mindset of the CT role attitude, this is a weak skill in keeping agreements with people.

As a phobic mindset, this explains why marshals tend to lack a sense of ethics. They have the potential to offend others due to a weak moral code. On the other hand, they are seldom a wimp with their social and career goals.

Hence, EH is the timid mindset of the marshal that forgets about ethics in their goals. They will avoid doing the right thing in situations. They are more concerned with just reacting.

### ATTITUDE ANALYSIS: SUPER-ID BLOCK

### 5. SUBDUED DREAMER - REALITY DISTILLATION (RD)
"...TO GET TO THE ROOT OF REALITY..."

Reality Distillation is the fifth irrational attitude. It is one-half of the super-id, the conscience of the id. For the marshal, this mindset is restless in the revealing of core truths. The conscious attitudes have sought action with knowledge. The RD attitude equates to the inner need to get to the root of reality. This swayable attitude may not ask for help in seeking the essence of issues.

Hence, RD is a dormant attitude that wants to discern the spirit of truth. A person with a strong conscious RD attitude can provoke a restart of this desire.

## 6. HIDDEN MOTIVATOR - SOCIAL INTEREST (SI)
### "...VALUE A LIFE WITH PEOPLE..."

Social Interest is the sixth rational attitude. It is the second half of the super-id, the conscience of the id. For the marshal, it yields results of the RD attitude by valuing relations. This attitude does not judge reality well until helped by someone with SI as a conscious attitude.

As the hidden agenda of the marshal, they may like to value a life with people more. They may need help with this weak area of their subconscious mind.

Hence, SI is the weak attitude that wants to relate socially and build a following. For example, the marshal may from time to time bring people together on the social scene.

## ATTITUDE ANALYSIS: ID BLOCK

## 7. DATA RECORDER - DYNAMIC STABILIZATION (DS)
### "...TRIED AND TESTED TACTICS..."

Dynamic Stabilisation is the seventh irrational attitude. It is one-half of the id, the most instinctual self. As we delve into the core of the marshal's mind, we find concern for anchoring to the known. The DS mindset will fulfil itself under periods of stress or upset. For example, under pressure, they may choose tried and tested tactics to achieve a goal.

Hence, DS is a strong subconscious mindset that provides the marshal on a whim to make sense of chaotic reality. They may use this skill to stay focused on methods that they know ought to work.

## 8. NATURAL ARTISAN - PRACTICAL RESULTS (PR)
### "...AN AUTOMATIC ZEST FOR BUSINESS LOGIC..."

Practical Results is the eighth rational attitude. It is the second half of the id, the most instinctual self. At the core of the marshal's mind, we find an automatic zest for business logic. Any goals in the world call for a practical system. This attitude keeps them tuned to knowing what works and what does not in their constant campaign with life.

Hence, PR is a strong subconscious mindset that keeps the marshal on the lookout for results. Therefore, they can make excellent additions to a sales force.

### PERSONAL DEVELOPMENT FOR ESTP'S

Marshals tend to act highly impulsive. They know how to do the required actions to get results. They have weak ethics. They like results at any cost. I suggest that they learn to develop a strong moral code as not to offend others on their journey up the corporate ladder.

Marshals tend to seek out people to build a following. This can make them seem narcissistic. They enjoy gaining respect from others. However, they do not always find the right emotional distance from people. I suggest that they embrace their spiritual development and learn to tone down their inherent egotism.

Marshals often do very well in their career goals. They have a mindset that allows them to push forward regardless of previous upsets. They do not like to look back at the past in worry. They live firmly in the here and now. I suggest that they learn the art of introspection to aid their skill to learn from their mistakes.

### FAMOUS EXAMPLES OF ESTP'S

- Donald Trump (American Industrialist)
- Steven Seagal (American Actor)
- George Bush, Jr. (43rd US President)
- Winston Churchill (British Politician)

# THE GAMMA QUADRA

Summary:
- Intellectual Age: middle-aged/adulthood
- Group Mantra: constant and never-ending industrialisation
- Stimulus: materialistic happiness
- Typical behaviour: driven, efficient, sociable
- Social Role: capitalists/political-marketers/criticise and remove the flaws and mistakes of the past
- Political philosophy: big collectivism/collective of corporations
- Epistemology: atheism/rationalism/empirical beliefs
- Moral dilemma: Can we all just get along peacefully and productively for the greater good?

Members:
- The "ISFj" Guardian
- The "ENTj" Pioneer
- The "ESFp" Ambassador
- The "INTp" Critic

A combination of SF's and NT's which translates to "Mature Socialisers" and "Adult Scientists" whom together form, in a nutshell, society's Peacemakers & Entrepreneurship division. The kind of people who want to see us live together harmoniously and reap the benefits of capitalism for the rest of the Socion.

## THE "ISFj" GUARDIAN

### OVERVIEW

The ISFj "Guardian" represents to me "the smooth operator" of the social neighbourhood. They use their charms to seduce others. These types cannot stand the thought of being alone. They often seek out people and relationships to support them.

Guardians usually have a traditional lifestyle. They have a desire for control. They love nothing more than to challenge the moral standards of others. They like to do everything by the book. They will bear any cause that grants security. They do not like to think for themselves.

Guardians tend to have unease on the subject of their fitness to deal with life's trials. They do not like to handle the complexities of modern life. They tend to support government programs that they believe will provide for their safety and needs. They are pleased to take a support role in any endeavour, working tirelessly to the end.

Guardians do not like change. They will resist new ways of doing things. They more often than not look for support roles in society that others avoid. They make great servants.

Guardians tend to fear disorderly conducts. They stand their ground with people and situations. They are hard to convince. They tend to be followers. They have an eagerness to help and nurture people.

## Model A: The "ISFj" Guardian

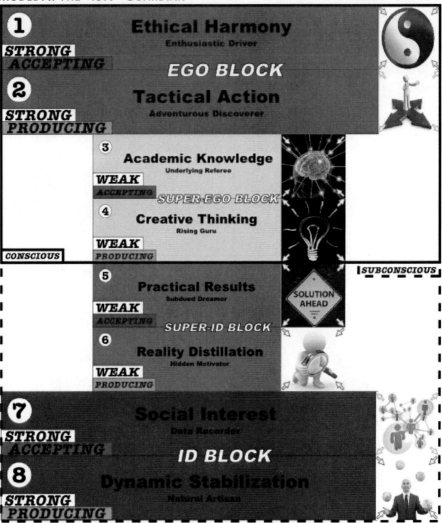

### Attitude Analysis: Ego Block

1. Enthusiastic Driver - Ethical Harmony (EH)
"...a life based on compassion..."

Ethical Harmony is the rational first attitude. This leads the guardian to the dominant stance that all that is manifesting is the expression of a soul or life force. All that happens is the result of a soul expressing its unique nature. Also, they live a life based on compassion – to see life as a huge clash between minds that are different.

Mature EH leads them to favour mercy for people who have done wicked acts, anything from theft to murder, etc. Under the universal laws that make the world safe, these actions would warrant jail time or the death sentence. From an EH view, the criminal is still a living person, thus precious in spite of what he did. If we walked in his shoes for a while, maybe we could see it his way. EH can look at how we could have done the same things under similar conditions. This use of sympathy leads to a firm tolerant mindset.

Guardians like to have compassion for others. They find something in their own heart that lets them see how someone could feel and act a particular way. They do this to feel hatred no longer or have a desire for revenge. For example, they can be first-rate jury members, as they like to debate a person's virtues. They are fair in their verdict even if the evidence leans towards a guilty one.

Hence, EH as the first attitude causes guardians to watch and live life as some soap opera. They usually create and live out intense dramas wherever they go.

## 2. Adventurous Discoverer - Tactical Action (TA)
### "...to perform tasks without thinking..."

Tactical Action is the irrational second attitude. It helps produce the insights of the EH attitude. In the world of public images, they find themselves with a topic to study and remark on. For example, they may talk about how some people are trying to look cool but failing.

To find a way for their primary moral perspectives to bear fruit they use TA. Their first EH attitude has led them to nurture a manner or charm. TA allows them to accept details as they appear. Also, they use their TA attitude to 'just react' to situations that require it. For example, on a night out they can seem to enjoy themselves in the moment.

Hence, TA as the second attitude provides the prompt to live life in the here-and-now based on a strong set of ethics. TA allows the guardian to perform tasks without thinking it through too much.

## ATTITUDE ANALYSIS: SUPER-EGO BLOCK

### 3. UNDERLYING REFEREE - ACADEMIC KNOWLEDGE (AK)
"...A SELF-ABSORBED FOCUS..."

Academic Knowledge is the third rational attitude. It is one-half of the super-ego and conscience behind the stronger ego attitudes. AK leads the guardian to reflect on his or her experiences. For example, now and then they need time alone to think about any problems they have.

AK leads the guardian to an immersed focus on their life experiences. They may do the same with other people who stand by them. If someone disagrees with them during a period of reflection, then they must be naive. They consider the other person wrong, as they do not understand their problems. They use this kind of narrow view often cynically.

As a complex, the guardian may act moody during their musings. This is due to a previous event that has questioned their high sense of ethics. We hint that it will be healthy for them to reflect in private through either writing or talking. Since they may not always find time to take needed leave, it can affect their general abilities. Until they can get over their anxious state, they will remain stressed by their problems. Thus, they tend to have a worry between moral resolve and corrupt conduct from others. Finally, they can represent the model parent since they have a well-built moral code.

In essence, the notion of being one's worst enemy brings knowledge as to why they acted and reacted to particular stimulus. If the Guardian considers this, they can learn to control their mind to avoid tense situations.

Yoga and meditation make useful healing for the Guardian. Though they do not deal directly with the cause, they can provide short-term relief. Ideally, they want the best of both worlds: internal mental control and external relaxation methods.

Hence, AK as the third attitude of the Guardian leads them to desire time to understand their problems. These directly relate to their morals and experiences in the real world.

### 4. RISING GURU - CREATIVE THINKING (CT)
*"...A WEAK DESIRE TO SEIZE OPPORTUNITIES..."*

Creative Thinking is the fourth irrational attitude. It is the second half of the super-ego and conscience behind the stronger ego attitudes. As the producing attitude for the AK attitude, it is the weak desire to see the potentials in the unknown. The guardian will avoid considering the trends in the world. They will prefer to stay grounded in reality.

As a phobic mindset, this explains why guardians can flock to the side at social events. With a weak need to seize chances, they might cease from moving to an open dance area where they might catch the interest of a prospective mate. The Rising Guru attitude needs a great passion for asserting itself. In the presence of others with the same weakness, they would feel at ease. Also, they would enjoy the presence of a type whose eighth attitude is their weakness.

Hence, CT is a timid attitude for the Guardian. It results in a lack of need to gain anything from detecting trends in society. For example, they may have many tangible skills, which remain hobbies since they rarely see how they could profit by it. Since they are seldom troubled by what could be, they tend to focus on what is thus having a liking to living life as realists. Thus, they make model supporters of any cause that take their interest. They may support a new venture or charity that requires steady work to achieve a goal.

### ATTITUDE ANALYSIS: SUPER-ID BLOCK

### 5. SUBDUED DREAMER - PRACTICAL RESULTS (PR)
*"...THE INNER NEED FOR SEEKING RESULTS..."*

Practical Results is the fifth rational attitude. It is one-half of the super-id, the conscience of the id. For the Guardian, this mindset is restless in the use of business sense to gain results. The conscious attitudes have built up strong ethics through many real-world experiences. The PR attitude equates to the inner need for seeking results. For example, finding a spouse by attending social events where there is likely to be prospects.

This swayable attitude may not ask for help in its private wish for results. For example, promotions at work may seldom concern them.

Hence, PR is a dormant attitude that wants them to achieve something useful with their lives. A person with a strong conscious PR attitude can provoke a restart of this desire.

### 6. HIDDEN MOTIVATOR - REALITY DISTILLATION (RD)
"...TO WEED THROUGH THE NONSENSE..."

Reality Distillation is the sixth irrational attitude. It is the second half of the super-id, the conscience of the id. For the Guardian, it yields results of the PR attitude by allowing them to weed through the fictions in reality. This attitude does not grasp truth well until helped by someone with RD as a conscious attitude.

As the hidden agenda of the guardian, they may like to weed through the nonsense in the world. They may need help with this weak area of their subconscious mind.

Hence, RD is the weak attitude that the world has many hurdles to the truth of a person or situation. For example, the guardian needs to know the crux of stuff devoid of confusion caused by irrelevant facts.

### ATTITUDE ANALYSIS: ID BLOCK

### 7. DATA RECORDER - SOCIAL INTEREST (SI)
"...TO APPRECIATE THE ROLES WE PLAY..."

Social Interest is the seventh rational attitude. It is one-half of the id, the most instinctual self. As we delve into the core of the guardian's mind, we find concern for a socially shared world. The SI mindset will fulfil itself under periods of stress or upset. For example, at a funeral, they play music that the guardian seals in their mind for the event. When the guardian listens to the music later, they will recall the event.

Hence, SI is a strong subconscious mindset that provides the guardian on a whim to appreciate the roles we play. They tend to value the treasures of the past more so than the mystery of the future.

## 8. Natural Artisan - Dynamic Stabilization (DS
"...AWARE OF SOCIAL NORMS AT ALL TIMES..."

Dynamic Stabilization is the irrational eighth attitude. It is the second half of the id, the most instinctual self. At the core of the guardian's mind, we find an automatic zest for firmness. Any conduct perceived by them as odd threatens the status quo. This attitude keeps them aware of social norms at all times. Any act deemed in violation of their old school values does not tolerate well.

Hence, DS is a strong subconscious mindset that keeps the guardian fixed to a firm reality. Therefore, they without a shred of doubt define for themselves and others what they see as 'normal'.

## PERSONAL DEVELOPMENT FOR ISFJ'S

Guardians are usually realists. They take up support roles in society. With a high need for firmness, those who do not obey the rules of social norms have an effect on them very easily. While they make excellent by the book people, they have difficulty thinking outside the box. I suggest that they learn to think laterally by appreciating the art of mind mapping as part of the planning process.

Anxiety can be a problem for the Guardian. They want to control every little bit of chaos. From young children who cause a mess in the kitchen to disorderly teenagers, they have a need for control. I suggest that they recognise their need to keep everything in order and let loose a bit.

With their strong id, guardians are quick to judge people based on first impressions. For example, if a person acted a certain way when they first met them it may take a long time to shake up their opinions. I suggest that they put their feelings aside when dealing with people and learn to see things more objectively.

### FAMOUS EXAMPLES OF ISFJ'S

- William Shatner (Canadian Actor)
- Sir Michael Caine, CBE (English Actor)
- Bob Gunton (American Actor)
- Elijah Wood (American Actor)

## THE "ENTJ" PIONEER

### OVERVIEW

The ENTj "Pioneer" represents to me "the Tony Stark" (from the Iron Man films/comics) of the social world. He takes great pleasure approaching each goal as a combat mission. He uses mental tactics to achieve his ends.

Pioneers are sharp at knowing the actions of others in advance. He can effectively get other people to do whatever he or she wants. He does this by the sheer force of his personality and through pressure. This makes him an excellent chess player. We often consider him as one of society's "bad boys".

Pioneers are mostly friendly people who put on the visage of a jerk. They do this to make up for their weak ethical attitudes. They have a fascination with the use of force, weapons, and martial arts. The quote that best describes them goes a bit like, "Power tends to corrupt, and absolute power corrupts absolutely. Great men are almost always bad men." Thus, their attitude towards work and all of life equates to strategic combat. They advocate the struggle to acquire and keep power.

Pioneers have a stern nature. They will reprimand cheating from others. They tend to have an obsessed view towards any disputes. They see this as a personal attack on them. They think they know best for all and sundry. The Frank Sinatra song, "My Way!" embodies this mindset.

Pioneers maintain a final agenda in spite of the methods they might use to reach their goals. They have weak ethics and a lack of introspection. This puts them at risk of giving in to corrupt habits say in business.

Pioneers act with a wild confidence. They enjoy quick movement in the direction of their goals. They have a desire to test the limits of applied theory.

## MODEL A: THE "ENTJ" PIONEER

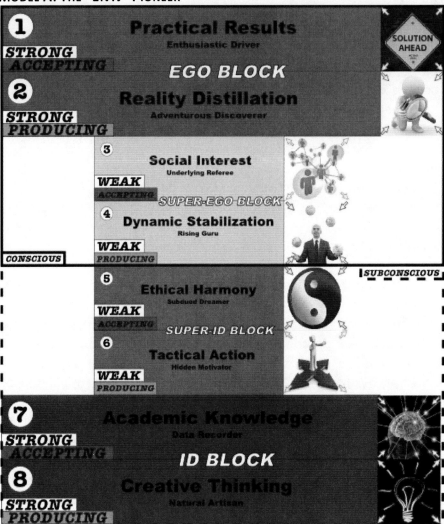

**ATTITUDE ANALYSIS: EGO BLOCK**

1. ENTHUSIASTIC DRIVER - PRACTICAL RESULTS (PR)
"...A FOCUS ON RESULTS..."

Practical Results is the rational first attitude. This leads the Pioneer to make consistent choices. They want deliverables such as those good for business. They value a process that will persist. A process that repeats is valuable from a PR view. This enables them to have useful options with others. There will be no doubt, as to whether each party has fulfilled its part of an agreement. This is because there is a focus on results. It is not about who is correct, as that would lead to an endless contest for the sake of it thus stagnating a project.

The pioneer can keep their promises using their strong PR mindset. On the other hand, they do not value ethics well. Honesty is not always their best rule. They concern themselves more with achieving results, not who is right or wrong. PR integrity means sticking with a project until they do it right. Either that or they quit when those they are working with interfering with their ability to do it right. In other words, they have no time for those who waste theirs when critical business goals at stake.

A mature pioneer is not troubled to drop workers who do not perform. Those who keep failing to perform at their job will likely lead to the conclusion that the job was not right for them in the first place. Hence, PR as the main mindset explains why pioneers more often than not make up a share of the world's entrepreneurs. They achieve results first and place ethics second.

## 2. ADVENTUROUS DISCOVERER - REALITY DISTILLATION (RD)
"...THE ART OF NEGOTIATION..."

Reality Distillation is the irrational second attitude. It helps turn out the results of the PR mindset by weeding out the distortions in reality. RD hones the pioneer's skill to negotiate the social world. He can exploit the assumptions that people make about him. Also, he makes an excellent marketing expert who knows how to draw attention to himself. He knows how to show his values to others. By letting others make guesses toward his veneer, he will be in due course gaining rapport. It then becomes a case of, is he who he presents himself to be? This may surprise others to know. For example, a group may see him as shrewd and ruthless though it may turn out that he is a beautiful person.

RD steers talks with others. It allows the pioneer to be on his guard against frauds. He can prevail by setting knots and traps for others to fall hooked on. He may also guide debates with others to commit to a vision that might not seem viable. Also, he plays his social life like a game of chess where he has already seen the endgame. Like a real leader, he lets others think they have won during the midgame while he directs the desired outcomes. As a long-range thinker, he has clearly defined outcomes for the game.

Hence, RD is the mindset that supports the pioneer using the art of negotiation. For example, he knows that wearing a smart suit equates to gaining instant respect from others.

## ATTITUDE ANALYSIS: SUPER-EGO BLOCK

### 3. UNDERLYING REFEREE - SOCIAL INTEREST (SI)
"...THE ROLES WE PLAY IN A SOCIALLY SHARED WORLD..."

Social Interest is the third rational attitude. It is one-half of the super-ego and conscience behind the stronger ego attitudes. SI concerns itself with the roles we play in a socially shared world. The pioneer views all from the homeless to those in work as having a dream. He needs to fulfil those dreams for the benefit of the world as a whole. He believes that this will end global poverty. This results in his role as a business leader in most places. For example, he enjoys social meetings aimed at getting things done. He does not mind taking centre stage as a sponsor of free enterprise.

SI leads the Pioneer to point others in the right course of action through his gift of leadership. He likes to make winners of others by getting them to copy his successes.

As a complex, the pioneer may get cranky when others try to question his guidance. They wish to make gainful results straight away. As long as he remains calm and collected, others will respect him. If he gets angry and loses focus for too long others will doubt his leadership.

Hence, SI as the third attitude of the pioneer leads him to value people well enough to guide them. He is skilled in the art of leading which equates to getting others to do things because they want to.

## 4. RISING GURU - DYNAMIC STABILIZATION (DS)
### "...A DISREGARD FOR THE APPARENT CHAOS..."

Dynamic Stabilization is the fourth irrational attitude. It is the second half of the super-ego and conscience behind the stronger ego attitudes. As the producing mindset for the SI attitude, it is the weak need to anchor to known customs in the world. The pioneer pays no attention to the chaos in the world. He will actively take risks where the average person will not.

As a phobic mindset, this explains why pioneers tend to ignore tried and tested ways that get results. They do not mind selling new concepts away from usual methods. For example, they make public a new piece of software, and people then have to buy a new PC to use it. This illustrates how they like to test the limits of new ideas.

Pioneers know how to bring results that build wealth. They tend to be masters of big business. They will not remain satisfied with a single source of income. If you work for a large corporation, it is likely that a pioneer runs it.

Hence, DS is the timid mindset of the pioneer that does not want to agree to proven means where they seek results. They will find new ways of doing business. For example, I have found a lot of them caught up in the network marketing industry.

### ATTITUDE ANALYSIS: SUPER-ID BLOCK

## 5. SUBDUED DREAMER - ETHICAL HARMONY (EH)
### "...TO DO THE RIGHT THING..."

Ethical Harmony is the fifth rational attitude. It is one-half of the super-id, the conscience of the id. For the pioneer, this mindset is restless in the use of morals to keep harmony. The conscious attitudes have sought no-nonsense results with the art of give and take. The EH attitude equates to the inner need for finding results in a right way.

This swayable attitude may not ask for help on the subject of ethics in the wake of their conscious actions. For example, charging high prices for their goods may seldom concern them.

Hence, EH is a dormant attitude that wants to do the right thing with their business. A person with a strong conscious EH attitude can provoke a restart of this desire.

## 6. HIDDEN MOTIVATOR - TACTICAL ACTION (TA)
### "...TO REACT TO THE WORLD..."

Tactical Action is the sixth irrational attitude. It is the second half of the super-id, the conscience of the id. For the pioneer, it yields results of the EH attitude by allowing them to react with no fear of the past or future. This attitude does not get going until helped by someone with TA as a conscious attitude.

As the hidden agenda of the pioneer; they may like to react to the world in a pragmatic way. They may need help with this weak area of their subconscious mind.

Hence, TA is the weak attitude that the world requires a no-nonsense reaction to it. For example, the Pioneer needs to live more in the here and now to benefit their sought results.

### ATTITUDE ANALYSIS: ID BLOCK

## 7. DATA RECORDER - ACADEMIC KNOWLEDGE (AK)
### "...A NEED FOR REFLECTION..."

Academic Knowledge is the seventh rational attitude. It is one-half of the id, the most instinctual self. As we delve into the core of the pioneer's mind, we find a need for reflection. The AK mindset will fulfil itself under periods of stress or upset. For example, after a failed venture they will want to understand why. They will eventually conclude that a lack of understanding in the first place may have played a part in his failures.

Hence, AK is the strong subconscious mindset that provides the pioneer with the whim to introspect. Over time, he will collect and store knowledge of systems, people, etc.

## 8. Natural Artisan - Creative Thinking (CT)
### "...an automatic zest for new opportunities..."

Creative Thinking is the irrational eighth attitude. It is the second half of the id, the most instinctual self. At the core of the pioneer's mind, we find an automatic zest for new opportunities. The status quo is never enough. There is always something he can do better, faster or more efficiently.

Hence, CT is a strong subconscious mindset that keeps the pioneer exposed to the 'big picture'. This fuels his capitalist spirit. He does not find it difficult to see the potential for wealth generation in the world.

### Personal development for ENTJ's

Pioneers have a drive to do well in business and life. The issue with their internal focus is that they tend to push people hard to get results. For example, in the network marketing industry, I find them at the top of their wealth building game. They like to assume that everyone can do well as they did. They quickly forget that while the system may be 'perfect' people are not as this book conveys. I suggest that they learn to realise the differences in individuals and adjust their expectations accordingly.

Pioneers who learn the art of introspection will boost their goals. They can focus on the wider issues and not just their drive to generate wealth. Those who build up their ethics can create wealth in ways that are more beneficial to themselves and others. By default, though, they can be ruthless to the point of others classing them as the "sharks of business". I suggest that they learn to appreciate people as "people" and not just impersonal objects ripe for their shrewd exploitation.

### Famous examples of ENTJ's
- Lord Alan Sugar (British Entrepreneur)
- Robert Downey, Jr. (American Actor)
- Quentin Tarantino (American Film Director)
- Larry Ellison (American Entrepreneur)

## THE "INTP" CRITIC

### OVERVIEW

The INTp "Critic" represents to me "The Architect" as a man who loves problem-solving. He directs his interests toward the harmonising of the hectic world. He has a mysterious need to find order out of disorder. He has a talent for lateral thinking. He has a grandiose vision of a better tomorrow for all.

Critics spend much time alone. They contemplate how to capitalise on the abundant resources of men's minds. They do this to make positive contributions to the world. His facade is cold and calm. His inner shell is warm and kind. He bears the burden of seeing society's problems. He longs to do something about them.

Critics have a mantra that would go a bit like, "If today were perfect there would be no need for tomorrow". They need to find an existing demand and create a market. They need to place themselves as one of the major suppliers of some item. Lastly, they need to convince people that they need it, or something bad will happen.

Critics make good task managers. They tend to live far away on a secluded island. From there they will create a healthy profit margin. This is where profits exceed costs. They will help deliver a global product that turns out a constant stream of benefits. They expect to have many repeat clients. Lastly, they will pay a sales force with replies prepared for any doubts.

Critics will reflect on the global market. This lets them build a big business that will continue far into the future. They want to retire in the knowledge that others will take care of their business after they have left. They will seek out a skilled person with steady and active leadership to succeed him or her.

Critics act goofy at times. They do not reveal much of their "inner life". They are engrossed in the right course of action. They have a slothful ease and a tongue in cheek attitude.

## MODEL A: THE "INTP" CRITIC

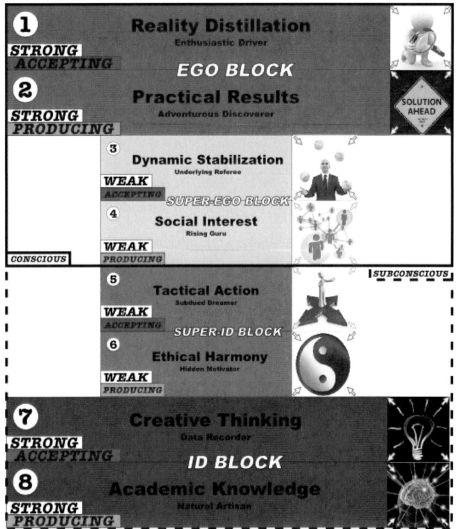

### ATTITUDE ANALYSIS: EGO BLOCK

1. ENTHUSIASTIC DRIVER - REALITY DISTILLATION (RD)
"...TO STRIP THINGS DOWN TO THEIR ESSENCE..."

Reality Distillation is the irrational first attitude. It leads the critic to see through the distortions present in reality, to see core truths. RD is a way for the critic to bypass extra details. He has a gift for getting to the crux of things.

Critics have the knack to see all the way down to basic reality. This can be a source of their sarcasm and ironic wit. Also, RD can make them seem to others as autistic. In truth, this is a good sign that they hold back a naive ingenuity.

Hence, RD as the first mindset of the critic allows him to get to the root truths. He knows how to strip things down to their essence.

### 2. Adventurous Discoverer - Practical Results (PR)
#### "...turn dreams into reality..."

Practical Results is the rational second attitude. It yields results of the RD mindset by giving the critic the skill to turn core truths into profits. They can boast many schemes in which to develop into goods. They have a vision for profit that drives them. They will get rid of many ideas that are not viable. With no trouble, they take on the role of entrepreneur.

Critics in business do not need a head office to get on track. They will keep costs to a minimum. For them, the thought is more key than the concrete aspects of running a company. The company is a concept that they value and use as a 'vehicle' to achieve their goals.

Hence, PR as the second mindset of the critic lets them turn dreams into reality. They know the value of a good idea and are not afraid to market it.

### Attitude Analysis: Super-Ego Block

### 3. Underlying Referee - Dynamic Stabilization (DS)
#### "...to develop intelligent ideas..."

Dynamic Stabilization is the third irrational attitude. It is one-half of the super-ego and conscience behind the stronger ego attitudes. DS lets the critic anchor to the tried and tested. They may decide to develop intelligent ideas that must work. They prefer to market themselves with well drawn out plans.

Critics have a weak need to stabilise reality to the known. They enjoy a sense of routine in business. Also, we might find them dressed in the same clothes repeatedly as a form of uniform.

Hence, DS as the third mindset defines the man behind the mask. The critic has a clear plan for their retirement. Therefore, it suits them to wonder when they will give up work, not if.

## 4. RISING GURU - SOCIAL INTEREST (SI)
"...A TIMID NEED TO NETWORK WITH PEOPLE..."

Social Interest is the fourth rational attitude. It is the second half of the super-ego and conscience behind the stronger ego attitudes. As the producing mindset for the DS attitude, this weak need accepts the roles we play in the socially shared world. The critic has a timid need to network with people.

As a phobic mindset, this explains why critics tend to tire easily of social contact. They do not like outside visitors who can disturb them. On the other hand, they require isolation to best figure out how to build wealth.

Hence, SI is the timid mindset of the critic that does not want to relate with others. He will avoid social events if he can help it.

## ATTITUDE ANALYSIS: SUPER-ID BLOCK

## 5. SUBDUED DREAMER - TACTICAL ACTION (TA)
"...THE INNER NEED FOR TAKING ACTION..."

Tactical Action is the fifth irrational attitude. It is one-half of the super-id, the conscience of the id. For the critic, this mindset is restless in the use of sensible reactions. The conscious attitudes have sought core truths with practical results. The TA attitude equates to the inner need for taking action to get those results. This swayable attitude may not ask for help in how to act more proactive.

Hence, TA is a dormant attitude that wants hands-on results. A person with a strong conscious TA attitude can provoke a restart of this desire.

## 6. HIDDEN MOTIVATOR - ETHICAL HARMONY (EH)
"...TO MAINTAIN SOCIAL HARMONY..."

Ethical Harmony is the sixth rational attitude. It is the second half of the super-id, the conscience of the id. For the critic, it yields results of the TA attitude given the concord between them and others. This attitude does not work well with ethics until helped by someone with EH as a conscious attitude.

As the hidden agenda of the critic, they may like to build a strong moral code. This will help them when dealing with others. They may need help with this weak area of their subconscious mind.

Hence, EH is the weak attitude that wants to maintain social harmony. For example, the critic needs to view people in a more caring way rather than as minor things.

**ATTITUDE ANALYSIS: ID BLOCK**

### 7. DATA RECORDER - CREATIVE THINKING (CT)
"...A NEED FOR TREND FORECASTING..."

Creative Thinking is the seventh irrational attitude. It is one-half of the id, the most instinctual self. As we delve into the core of the critic's mind, we find a need for trend forecasting. The CT mindset will fulfil itself under periods of stress or upset. For example, they may start to get new insights when drunk.

Hence, CT is the strong subconscious mindset that provides the critic with the whim to notice the 'big picture'. Over time, they will collect and store many bright ideas.

### 8. NATURAL ARTISAN - ACADEMIC KNOWLEDGE (AK)
"...AN AUTOMATIC ZEST FOR DEEP UNDERSTANDING..."

Academic Knowledge is the eighth rational attitude. It is the second half of the id, the most instinctual self. At the core of the critic's mind, we find an automatic zest for deep understanding. He may know any area of interest well. For example, he may have knowledge of computer design letting him build his systems.

Hence, AK is the strong subconscious mindset that provides the critic with the art of introspection. This fuels his progressive views on doing business. He does not find it difficult to learn from past mistakes.

### PERSONAL DEVELOPMENT FOR INTP'S

Critics have a weak TA mindset. They do not value the sensory world. This may result in not taking care of their bodies. I suggest that they start an exercise program. This should allow them to escape from living in their minds.

Critics have a strong CT mindset. They enjoy long-range thinking. This may result in not wanting to deal with mundane tasks. For example, they will do everything that needs doing providing they know it is conducive to their success. I suggest that the critic finds and sets up a system to ease the process of getting things done.

Critics have a weak SI mindset. They are timid by nature. This may result in not dealing with people well. I suggest that they brush up on their social skills. This should allow them to become gregarious.

### FAMOUS EXAMPLES OF INTP'S

- Bill Gates (American Industrialist)
- Charles Darwin (British Naturalist)
- J. K. Rowling, OBE (British Author)
- Warren Buffet (American Investor)
- Felix Dennis (British Industrialist & Author)

## THE "ESFP" AMBASSADOR

### OVERVIEW

The ESFp "Ambassador" represents to me "the Don Juan" of the free world. She has an urge for contacts and a dislike of being alone. She feels a loving and focused attachment in her relationships. She displays an outgoing, hasty, and joyful life. She is undaunted by taking risks.

Ambassadors are friendly with an outward zest. They live life as an adventure. They feel alive! They bring smiles to other people with light-hearted jokes.

Ambassadors back the policy of free will. They take pleasure in many freedoms. They like reckless actions. They make good performers. Ambassadors have a wealth of extroversion where they cannot spend much time alone. They enjoy others spotting them with their vivid displays of passion. They want others to meet their needs. They put out great efforts to avoid rejection.

Ambassadors have a lack of introversion where they cannot take much time to think about their lives in depth. They end up with chronic feelings of emptiness. They may be prone to self-destructive behaviours.

Ambassadors have much grace even though they can act playful. They are usually well known. They enjoy being the centre of attention. Lastly, they like to have hands-on involvement in the world around them.

## MODEL A: THE "ESFP" AMBASSADOR

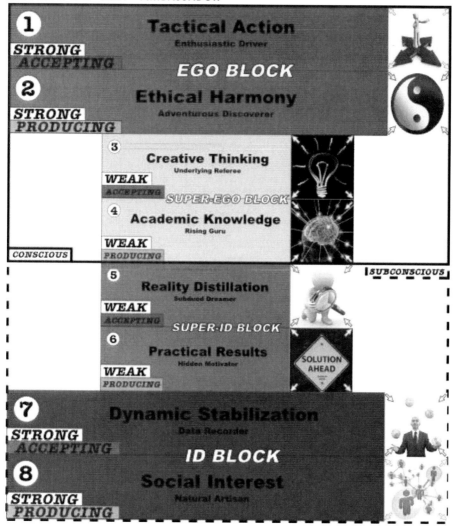

## ATTITUDE ANALYSIS: EGO BLOCK

### 1. ENTHUSIASTIC DRIVER - TACTICAL ACTION (TA)
"...TO SEE THE WORLD AS-IS..."

Tactical Action is the irrational first attitude. It leads the ambassador to see the world as-is. All is clear needing no explanation. They live close to nature. They naturally react to the details in the world. They are not deep thinkers. They do not live in a world of theory.

Hence, TA as the first mindset of the ambassador lets them live life without much thought. For example, they may form many relationships on a whim. They tend to react more than think.

## 2. ADVENTUROUS DISCOVERER - ETHICAL HARMONY (EH)
### "...A STRONG SENSE OF ETHICS..."

Ethical Harmony is the rational second attitude. It yields results of the TA attitude by adding a strong sense of ethics when dealing with people. The ambassador brings harmony to a place through their moral codes. For example, as an actor, they may deliver value for all by way of amusement.

Hence, EH as the second mindset of the ambassador provides the morals in their affairs with others. For example, they may call a truce between two opposing parties.

**ATTITUDE ANALYSIS: SUPER-EGO BLOCK**

## 3. UNDERLYING REFEREE - CREATIVE THINKING (CT)
### "...TO SPOT POTENTIAL WAYS TO BRING HARMONY..."

Creative Thinking is the third irrational attitude. It is one-half of the super-ego and conscience behind the stronger ego attitudes. CT is a way for the ambassador to spot potential ways to bring harmony. For example, they see a gap in the market for a TV program that fills an entertainment need.

Ambassadors have a week need to see the 'big picture'. They may have many ideas to make them better at diplomacy. Also, we might find them keeping informed of current affairs.

Hence, CT as the third mindset defines the man behind the mask. The ambassador has a directive to seek out new diplomatic relations. Therefore, it suits them to have a large circle of contacts.

## 4. RISING GURU - ACADEMIC KNOWLEDGE (AK)
### "...A WEAK SKILL FOR REFLECTION..."

Academic Knowledge is the fourth rational attitude. It is the second half of the super-ego and conscience behind the stronger ego attitudes. As the producing mindset of the CT attitude, this is a weak skill for reflection.

As a phobic mindset, this explains why ambassadors tend to lack in-depth thoughts. They view life as thrilling that calls for a minimal study. On the other hand, they require introspection to teach new subjects that take their interest.

Hence, AK is the timid mindset of the ambassador who does not want to go back to school so to speak. They will avoid philosophical debates if they can help it.

**ATTITUDE ANALYSIS: SUPER-ID BLOCK**

5. SUBDUED DREAMER - REALITY DISTILLATION (RD)
"...THE INNER NEED TO GET THE ROOT OF REALITY..."

Reality Distillation is the fifth irrational attitude. It is one-half of the super-id, the conscience of the id. For the ambassador, this mindset is restless in the revealing of core truths. The conscious attitudes have sought action with harmony. The RD attitude equates to the inner need to get the root of reality. This swayable attitude may not ask for help in finding the essence of issues.

Hence, RD is a dormant attitude that wants to discern the spirit of truth. A person with a strong conscious RD attitude can provoke a restart of this desire.

6. HIDDEN MOTIVATOR - PRACTICAL RESULTS (PR)
"...TO GET RESULTS..."

Practical Results is the sixth rational attitude. It is the second half of the super-id, the conscience of the id. For the ambassador, it yields results of the RD attitude by converting core truths into profits. This attitude does not work well in gaining results until helped by someone with PR as a conscious attitude.

As the hidden agenda of the ambassador, they may like to build wealth. This will assist them in turning dreams into reality. They may need help with this weak area of their subconscious mind.

Hence, PR is the weak attitude that wants to get results. For example, the ambassador needs to change their arty ways into a profitable scheme.

## ATTITUDE ANALYSIS: ID BLOCK

### 7. DATA RECORDER - DYNAMIC STABILIZATION (DS)
"...TO PLAY SAFE IN THE WORLD..."

Dynamic Stabilization is the seventh irrational attitude. It is one-half of the id, the most instinctual self. As we delve into the core of the ambassador's mind, we find a need for anchoring to the tried and tested.

The DS mindset will fulfil itself under periods of stress or upset. For example, they may make judgments towards the environment that do not change for a time.

Hence, DS is the strong subconscious mindset that provides the ambassador with the whim to play safely in the world. Over time, they will collect and store many details about the surrounding chaos.

### 8. NATURAL ARTISAN - SOCIAL INTEREST (SI)
"...AN AUTOMATIC ZEST FOR SOCIALISM..."

Social Interest is the eighth rational attitude. It is the second half of the id, the most instinctual self. At the core of the ambassador's mind, we find an automatic zest for socialism. She may know all about equity and fairness. For example, she may host a diplomatic party with the aim of getting a group of people to unite in a common goal.

Hence, SI is the strong subconscious mindset that makes the ambassador a people person. This fuels her need to socialise often. She does not find it difficult to relate to others.

## PERSONAL DEVELOPMENT FOR ESFP'S

Ambassadors lack a blueprint of how the social world works. They do not live in the world of theory; they live in the world of real life. I suggest they learn this subject to help their diplomatic skills.

Ambassadors have a weak skill to weed through the extra details in reality. They tend to judge people based on 'first impressions' alone. I suggest they take extra care in forming their relationships with others.

Ambassadors have a weak skill to get real world results. They do not tend to start businesses. I suggest they surround themselves with logical types to get started.

### FAMOUS EXAMPLES OF ESFP'S

- Tom Jones, OBE (Welsh Singer)
- Kevin Spacey (American Actor)
- Pam Grier (American Actress)
- Dean Cain (American Actor)

# THE DELTA QUADRA

Overview:
- Intellectual Age: old age/elder-hood
- Group Mantra: constant and never-ending indoctrination
- Stimulus: altruistic happiness
- Typical behaviour: serious, productive, communal
- Social Role: conservationists/religious-educators/ensuring a stable environment and source of resources
- Political philosophy: weak collectivism/collective of organisations
- Epistemology: theism/mysticism/irrational beliefs
- Moral dilemma: Why can't we all think the same to achieve a society that works in perfect order?

Members:
- The "INFj" Humanist
- The "ESTj" Director
- The "ENFp" Psychologist
- The "ISTp" Craftsman

A combination of NF's and ST's which translates to "Concerned Humanists" and "Elder Pragmatists" whom together form, in a nutshell, society's Conservationists & Community-Focused division. The kind of people who want to maintain a healthy world and promote sustainable living standards for the rest of the Socion.

## THE "INFJ" HUMANIST

### OVERVIEW

The INFj "Humanist" represents to me "the sensitive martyr" of the social world. He is always sacrificing himself in some way. He is touchy and prone to socially avoidant behaviour. He does not like when others scorn his ideas.

Humanists are hopeless romantics longing for things they cannot have. They can get into disturbing rows with others. Thus, they get upset with no trouble. They find themselves at risk sexually and expect someone to teach them the basics. They are always searching for that ideal partner. They are rarely satisfied.

Humanists work long and hard in their career. They have traits akin to Avoidant Personality Disorder (AvPD). They strive to reach a corporate position that allows them to work from the safety of their office away from anyone who can upset them. They can promise one thing, like a call back to discuss an interview and end up doing something avoidant instead, like sending their feedback in an email.

Humanists use positive thinking to pilot their world. They love to live in a dream world. They believe that life can be a perfect utopia and so wonderful. On the other hand, they have an ongoing fight with existential despair and feelings of worthlessness.

Humanists tend to be gentle with firm principles. They like to show a positive attitude. They like to share your world. They are also said to have a strong 'sixth sense' ability.

## MODEL A: THE "INFJ" HUMANIST

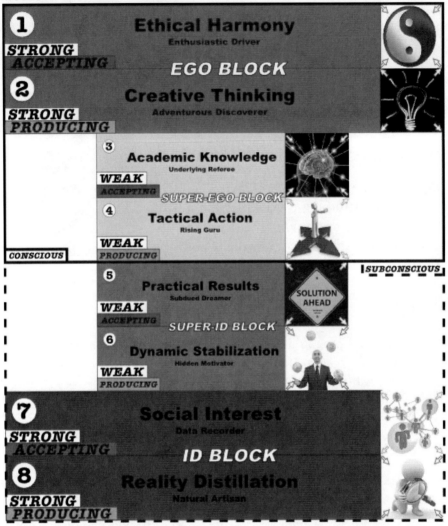

## ATTITUDE ANALYSIS: EGO BLOCK

1. ENTHUSIASTIC DRIVER - ETHICAL HARMONY (EH)
"...TO BE ON GUARD AGAINST DISCORD..."

Ethical Harmony is the rational first attitude. This leads the humanist to the dominant stance that all that is manifesting is the expression of a soul or life force. All that happens is the result of a soul expressing its unique nature. Also, they live a life of concern for the harmony between self and others.

Hence, EH as the main attitude causes humanists to be on guard against discord. They usually keep their distance from hostile social situations.

## 2. ADVENTUROUS DISCOVERER - CREATIVE THINKING (CT)
"...A REFLECTION OF A GREATER REALITY..."

Creative Thinking is the irrational second attitude. It helps produces results of the EH attitude. In the world of potentials, they find themselves with various trends to remark on. For example, they can spot by instinct when they think a person may be exhibiting signs of mental grief.

Humanists make model nurses. They know how to dig deep into the minds of others in a spiritual way. Thus, they have a knack for reading how others are feeling. For example, a person looks awkward at a social event. This may be a reflection of a greater reality i.e. the reality of their inner feelings.

Hence, CT as the second attitude provides the prompt to their moral codes to notice how people are feeling. CT allows the humanist to see the broader contexts in the world.

## ATTITUDE ANALYSIS: SUPER-EGO BLOCK

## 3. UNDERLYING REFEREE - ACADEMIC KNOWLEDGE (AK)
"...A SELF-ABSORBED FOCUS..."

Academic Knowledge is the third rational attitude. It is one-half of the super-ego and conscience behind the stronger ego attitudes. AK leads the humanist to reflect on his or her experiences. For example, they may like to ponder on what they have learnt about the psyche and their relationships.

AK leads the humanist to a self-absorbed focus on their life experiences. They may do the same with other people who stand by them. If someone disagrees with them during a period of reflection, then they must be naive. They consider the other person wrong, as they do not understand their problems. They use this kind of narrow view often cynically.

As a complex, the humanist may get irritable while going through a phase of reflection. This is due to a previous event that has questioned their strong sense of ethics.

Hence, AK as the third attitude of the humanist leads them to desire time to understand their problems. These directly relate to their morals and experiences in the real world.

### 4. RISING GURU - TACTICAL ACTION (TA)
#### "...A LATE DEVELOPER IN LIFE..."
Tactical Action is the fourth irrational attitude. It is the second half of the super-ego conscience behind the stronger ego attitudes. As the producing attitude for the AK attitude, it is the weak desire to react to the world in a no-nonsense way. The humanist will avoid living in the here and now. He is usually a late developer in life as to pleasure seeking.

As a phobic mindset, this explains why humanists can have a carefully guarded fear of intimacy. They may prefer instead to uphold a healthy lifestyle. This is due to the weakness of this attitude.

Hence, TA is a timid attitude for the humanist. It results in a general withdrawal from living in the moment. Since they seldom focus on the here and now, they tend to live in the past or future.

### ATTITUDE ANALYSIS: SUPER-ID BLOCK

### 5. SUBDUED DREAMER - PRACTICAL RESULTS (PR)
#### "...THE INNER NEED FOR SEEKING RESULTS..."
Practical Results is the fifth rational attitude. It is one-half of the super-id, the conscience of the id. For the humanist, this mindset is restless in the use of business sense to gain results. The conscious attitudes have built up strong ethics through many real-world experiences. The PR attitude equates to the inner need for seeking results. For example, they may seldom concern themselves by freelance openings for building wealth.

This swayable attitude may not ask for help in its private wish for results. For example, they may not know well how to profit from their ethical outlooks.

Hence, PR is a dormant attitude that wants to achieve something useful with their lives. A person with a strong conscious PR attitude can provoke a restart of this desire.

### 6. HIDDEN MOTIVATOR - DYNAMIC STABILIZATION (DS)
"...TO STABILISE REALITY..."

Dynamic Stabilization is the sixth irrational attitude. It is the second half of the super-id, the conscience of the id. For the humanist, it yields results of the PR attitude by anchoring to the known. This mindset does not judge reality well until helped by someone with DS as a conscious attitude.

As the hidden agenda of the humanist, they may like to stabilise reality more. For example, they may like to live a healthier lifestyle. They may need help with this weak area of their subconscious mind.

Hence, DS is the weak attitude that the world is a jumble of chaotic things. For example, the humanist decides to avoid using certain products that have toxic ingredients.

### ATTITUDE ANALYSIS: ID BLOCK

### 7. DATA RECORDER - SOCIAL INTEREST (SI)
"...TO APPRECIATE THE ROLES WE PLAY..."

Social Interest is the seventh rational attitude. It is one-half of the id, the most instinctual self. As we delve into the core of the humanist's mind, we find concern for being part of a socially shared world. The SI mindset will fulfil itself under periods of stress or upset. For example, at a party, the humanist may feel pressurised to socialise.

Hence, SI is a strong subconscious mindset that provides the humanist on a whim to appreciate the roles we play. They tend to remain in the background.

## 8. NATURAL ARTISAN - REALITY DISTILLATION (RD)
### "...AN AUTOMATIC ZEST FOR SOUL SEARCHING..."

Reality Distillation is the irrational eighth attitude. It is the second half of the id, the most instinctual self. At the core of the humanist's mind, we find an automatic zest for soul searching. Any aspects of reality that seem distorted will go through a filtering process. This attitude keeps them aware of core truths at all times. They are skilled in the art of listening.

Hence, RD is a strong subconscious mindset that keeps the humanist aware of the root of reality. Therefore, they have a talent for discussing aspects of reality that others miss.

### PERSONAL DEVELOPMENT FOR INFJ'S

Humanists tend to put the needs of others before their own. They have an altruistic nature to a degree. They believe they are serving the world for a higher cause. I suggest that they learn to put their needs first.

Humanists tend to withdraw from living in the moment and accepting reality as-is. This leads them to concentrate on the future rather than the present. They may neglect their bodies as a result. I suggest that they learn to become present by doing more exercise. Also, they can learn meditation with such techniques as Yoga and Tai Chi.

Humanists tend to end up frail and vulnerable to external pressures. After living a life of servitude, they may have little to show for it except undue utopianism. They a child-like wonder and desire to achieve extroverted goals. I suggest that they learn about business and marketing. This will give them the practical tools to achieve their ideals.

### FAMOUS EXAMPLES OF INFJ'S

- Alice Cooper (American Rock Singer)
- Gary Craig (EFT Founder)
- Jacque Fresco (Creator of The Venus Project)

## THE "ESTj" DIRECTOR

### OVERVIEW

The ESTj "Director" represents to me "the beauty and the beast" of the social world. He alternates between hostile defiance and contrition. He has a pervasive pattern of pessimistic attitudes and a tremendous dedication to his career. He can be a workaholic.

Directors believe in their right to enjoy themselves on their terms in their own time. They value and protect their comfort, their free time, and their individual pursuit of happiness.

Directors have a passive-aggressive nature. This leads them to get peeved off with authority figures in their career thus steering them towards "be your boss" type roles. They believe they are self-sufficient and do not need others to help them reach their goals.

Directors make keen workers to a cause. They know how to resist the control of authorities while at the same time keeping their support and acceptance. This allows them to behave in a society like a good citizen and leave plenty of room for the pursuit of their needs. They will forcefully drag you along to where their adventures take them in the name of blasé pleasures.

Directors tend to be busy with projects. They are practical yet sceptical. They are action oriented. They are skilled. They like active involvement.

## MODEL A: THE "ESTJ" DIRECTOR

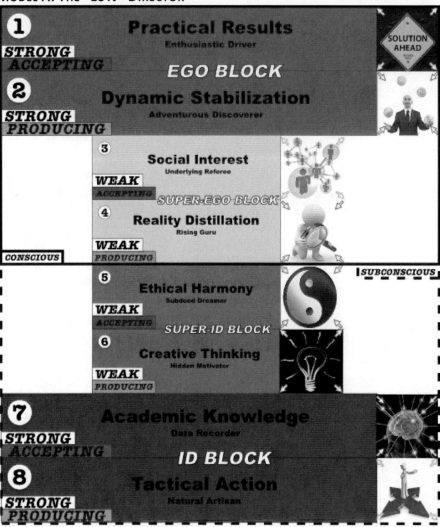

### ATTITUDE ANALYSIS: EGO BLOCK

1. ENTHUSIASTIC DRIVER - PRACTICAL RESULTS (PR)
*"...A FOCUS ON RESULTS..."*

Practical Results is the rational first attitude. This leads the director to make consistent choices. They want deliverables such as those good for business. They value a process that will persist. A process that repeats is valuable from a PR view. This enables them to have useful options with others. There will be no doubt, as to whether each party has fulfilled its part of an agreement. This is because there is a focus on results. It is not about who is correct, as that would lead to an endless contest for the sake of it thus stagnating a project.

The director is not attracted to sketchy ventures but in proven systems to get things done. This makes them magnificent in management although less open to new ways of doing things. For example, they would do well to run a franchise with predefined rules.

Hence, PR as the main mindset explains why directors more often than not make up a share of the world's small business owners. They achieve results first and place ethics second.

### 2. ADVENTUROUS DISCOVER - DYNAMIC STABILIZATION (DS)
*"...TO ALIGN THEM WITH WHAT IS KNOWN..."*

Dynamic Stabilization is the irrational second attitude. It helps produces results of the PR mindset by anchoring the director to the known. DS hones the director's skill to assess what works and what does not in the world. He can act as a wise business mentor. Also, he may have much experience of businesses that failed. This may have been due to common reasons he has indexed. Therefore, he has an old school nature regarding ideas for business.

DS makes the director risk adverse. Thus they tend to do well in small to medium sized organisations. Directors usually bring stability to an organisation after it is has been founded. They do not like to take large risks.

Hence, DS is the mindset that supports the director using stabilising reality. For example, they have a liking to working with systems that have been tried and tested.

**ATTITUDE ANALYSIS: SUPER EGO BLOCK**

### 3. UNDERLYING REFEREE - SOCIAL INTEREST (SI)
*"...THE ROLES WE PLAY IN A SOCIALLY SHARED WORLD..."*

Social Interest is the third rational attitude. It is one-half of the super-ego and conscience behind the stronger ego attitudes. SI concerns itself with the roles we play in a socially shared world. The director may like to host parties or run ventures that encourage a social theme. They will tend to have ideas for a business based on something communal. They will look to provide useful results to the local community in need of some service.

As a complex, the director may get cranky when people question his ideas for a business with a social premise. For example, he may decide to work for a local community centre. He does not expect others to grill his intentions.

Hence, SI as the third attitude of the director leads him to value people well enough to guide them. He is skilled in the art of managing which equates to taking on a mentor role with others.

## 4. RISING GURU - REALITY DISTILLATION (RD)
*"...TO SEE THROUGH THE DISTORTIONS OF REALITY..."*

Reality Distillation is the fourth irrational attitude. It is the second half of the super-ego and conscience behind the stronger ego attitudes. As the producing mindset for the SI attitude, it is the weak need to see through the distortions of reality. The director pays no attention to the core truths in the world. He will prefer observed evidence to half-baked conclusions.

Directors know how to bring results that build modest wealth. They tend to be masters of small business. They will not remain content by a low paid job.

Hence, RD is the timid mindset of the director that does not want to interpret reality fully. They will seek out old ways of doing business. For example, most bank managers tend to be directors. They mostly have a negative view of the future hence denying loans to start-ups that do not have clear business plans.

## ATTITUDE ANALYSIS: SUPER ID BLOCK

## 5. SUBDUED DREAMER - ETHICAL HARMONY (EH)
*"...TO DO THE RIGHT THING..."*

Ethical Harmony is the fifth rational attitude. It is one-half of the super-id, the conscience of the id. For the director, this mindset is restless in the use of morals to keep harmony. The conscious attitudes have sought tried and tested results. The EH attitude equates to the inner need for finding results in a good way.

This swayable attitude may not ask for help on the subject of ethics in the wake of their conscious actions. For example, denying loans to start-ups due to having dealt with many failed ventures in the past.

Hence, EH is a dormant attitude that wants to do the right thing. A person with a strong conscious EH attitude can provoke a restart of this desire.

### 6. Hidden Motivator - Creative Thinking (CT)
*"...to spot potentials in the world..."*

Creative Thinking is the sixth irrational attitude. It is the second half of the super-id, the conscience of the id. For the director, it yields results of the EH attitude by allowing them to see the 'big picture'. This attitude does not get going until help someone with CT as a conscious attitude.

As the hidden agenda of the director, they may like to spot potentials in the world. They may need help with this weak area of their subconscious mind.

Hence, CT is the weak attitude that the world has many possibilities therein. For example, rather than stick to the tried and tested the director could do well to listen to suggestions on new ways of doing business.

### Attitude Analysis: Id Block

### 7. Data Recorder - Academic Knowledge (AK)
*"...a need for reflection..."*

Academic Knowledge is the seventh rational attitude. It is one-half of the id, the most instinctual self. As we delve into the core of the director's mind, we find a need for reflection. The AK mindset will fulfil itself under periods of stress or upset. For example, they may force themselves to learn something to pass a test they need to pass to get a job.

Hence, AK is the strong subconscious mindset that provides the director with the whim to introspect. Over time, he will collect and store knowledge of systems, people, etc.

## 8. Natural Artisan - Tactical Action (TA)
### "...an automatic zest for pro-action..."

Tactical Action is the irrational eighth attitude. It is the second half of the id, the most instinctual self. At the core of the director's mind, we find an automatic zest for pro-action. He lives in the here and now. He knows how to adopt a can-do attitude.

Hence, TA is a strong subconscious mindset that keeps the director tuned into being action orientated. This fuels his capitalist spirit. He does not find it difficult to react to the world and get things done.

### Personal development for ESTJ's

Directors tend to be good middle managers. This is because they know how to get results in a tried and tested way. Since they lack seeing the 'big picture', they may miss opportunities for promotion. I suggest that they open their minds to global business to take their ventures to the next level.

Directors have the drive to do well in business and life. They are good at getting results. However, placing them in a mature company in a senior role is only good if the CEO wants them to maintain their department. They are not good at growing a business. They are slow to adopt new technologies and raise the industry standards. I suggest that they learn the art of brainstorming and mind mapping to become more open to new ideas and innovations.

### Famous examples of ESTJ's

- Thomas Edison (American Inventor)
- Steve Ballmer (American Businessman)
- Paul McKenna (English Hypnotist)
- Jeri Ryan (American Actress)

# THE "ISTP" CRAFTSMAN

## OVERVIEW

The ISTp "Craftsman" represents to me "the lone ranger" of the social world. They mostly have a failure to conform to social norms. Also, they have a pervasive pattern of impulsivity with an inability to plan.

Craftsmen have low extroversion. They choose loneliness. They have a lack of enthusiasm to assert themselves. They seldom take on management roles, even when trained. This is due to their social inhibitions and general shyness.

Craftsmen have a desire to create. This stems from an impulse to bring meaning from the chaotic world they perceive around them. They strive to acquire harmony and order in their world. They tend to have a high amount of anxiety.

Craftsmen have trouble with changing social conditions. They tend to be conservative with a low tolerance for diverse lifestyles. They also have a very narrow range of interests.

Craftsmen tend to have a soft blankness about them. They have an internal independence. They are hard to impress. They are not easily excited. Lastly, they are usually expressively cool and unknowable by others.

## MODEL A: THE "ISTP" CRAFTSMAN

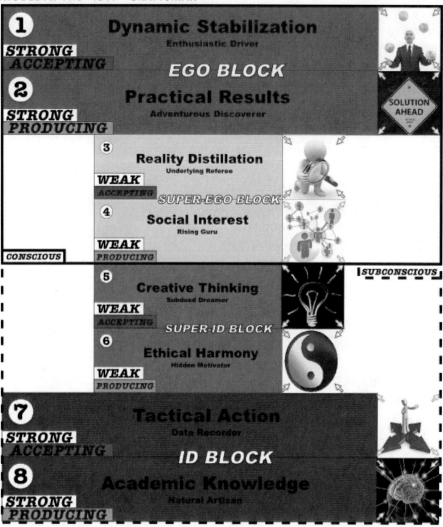

### ATTITUDE ANALYSIS: EGO BLOCK

1. ENTHUSIASTIC DRIVER - DYNAMIC STABILIZATION (DS)
"...TO CREATE ORDER OUT OF THE CHAOS OF LIFE..."

Dynamic Stabilisation is the irrational first attitude. It leads the craftsman to live in a world of always changing stimuli. Therefore, DS is like having a stabiliser system that with reality. He will even out reality and give it a consistent meaning for himself.

Hence, DS is a need to create order out of the chaos of life. It leads the craftsman to find one's feet in the world. They have a need to live a stress-free life with high peace of mind.

### 2. ADVENTUROUS DISCOVERER - PRACTICAL RESULTS (PR)
"...TO DO SOMETHING USEFUL..."

Practical Results is the rational second attitude. It helps produces results that the DS mindset needs. Common sense combines with a need for results. For example, crafting a statue out of stone as a way of creating something of meaning and value.

Hence, PR as the second attitude serves as a kind of prompt to the DS attitude that the world requires them to do something useful.

### ATTITUDE ANALYSIS: SUPER-EGO BLOCK

### 3. UNDERLYING REFEREE - REALITY DISTILLATION (RD)
"...TO DISCERN REALITY WITHOUT ANY FLUFF..."

Reality Distillation is the third irrational attitude. It is one-half of the super-ego and conscience behind the stronger ego attitudes. For the craftsman, seeking core truths does not show on the surface much. They tend to get to the root of reality behind the scenes. For example, they use this skill to be on guard against cheaters.

As a complex, the craftsman may become cross if not allowed to be outwardly artistic. He expects to make something useful out of a chaotic reality. He does not like others grilling him on his plans.

Hence, RD as the third attitude leads the craftsman to discern reality without any fluff. For example, he comments on a friend's relationship and tries to get to the root of how they feel about each other.

### 4. RISING GURU - SOCIAL INTEREST (SI)
"...A WEAK DESIRE FOR SOCIAL INTERACTION..."

Social Interest is the fourth rational attitude. It is the second half of the super-ego and conscience behind the stronger ego attitudes. As the producing attitude for the RD attitude, this weak need accepts the roles we play in the socially shared world. The craftsman has a weak desire for social interaction.

As a phobic mindset, this explains why craftsmen may find it terribly difficult to bond with others. They do not like outside visitors who can disturb them. On the other hand, they prefer isolation and work best alone.

Hence, SI is the timid mindset of the craftsman. It results in his enigmatic nature where they appear to keep their cool in most if not all situations.

**ATTITUDE ANALYSIS: SUPER-ID BLOCK**

### 5. SUBDUED DREAMER - CREATIVE THINKING (CT)
"...TO SEE THE 'BIG PICTURE'..."

Creative Thinking is the fifth irrational attitude. It is one-half of the super-id, the conscience of the id. For the craftsman, this mindset is restless in seeing the trends in the world. The conscious attitudes have sought upon making sense of a jumbled world. The CT attitude equates to the inner need to see the 'big picture'. For example, they may seldom wonder how they can use services to promote themselves better.

This swayable attitude may not ask for help in its private wish to see reality in a broad context. For example, after years of dealing with a chaotic world, they may wish to think more laterally.

Hence, CT is a dormant attitude that wants the craftsman to wonder what could be. A person with a strong conscious CT attitude can provoke a restart of this desire.

### 6. HIDDEN MOTIVATOR - ETHICAL HARMONY (EH)
"...TO MAINTAIN SOCIAL HARMONY..."

Ethical Harmony is the sixth rational attitude. It is the second half of the super-id, the conscience of the id. For the craftsman, it yields results of the CT attitude given the concord between them and others. This attitude does not work well with ethics until helped by someone with EH as a conscious attitude.

As the hidden agenda of the craftsman, they may like to build a strong moral code. This will help them when dealing with others. They may need help with this weak area of their subconscious mind.

Hence, EH is the weak attitude that wants to maintain social harmony. For example, the craftsman needs to view people in a more caring way rather than as minor things.

## ATTITUDE ANALYSIS: ID BLOCK

### 7. DATA RECORDER - TACTICAL ACTION (TA)
"...A NO-NONSENSE RESPONSE TO THE WORLD..."

Tactical Action is the seventh irrational attitude. It is one-half of the id, the most instinctual self. As we delve into the core of the craftsman's mind, we find concern for a no-nonsense response to the world. The TA mindset will fulfil itself under periods of stress or upset. For example, they may loosen up after a few drinks allowing them to live more in the moment.

Hence, TA is a strong subconscious mindset that provides the craftsman on a whim to take action. They may use this skill to keep their lives moving forward.

### 8. NATURAL ARTISAN - ACADEMIC KNOWLEDGE (AK)
"...AN AUTOMATIC ZEST FOR THOROUGH UNDERSTANDING..."

Academic Knowledge is the eighth rational attitude. It is the second half of the id, the most instinctual self. At the core of the craftsman's mind, we find an automatic zest for thorough understanding. He may know any area of interest well. For example, he may have highly specialised knowledge used for construction purposes.

Hence, AK is the strong subconscious mindset that provides the craftsman with the art of introspection. This fuels his progressive views of doing something practical. He does not find it difficult to learn from past mistakes.

## PERSONAL DEVELOPMENT FOR ISTP'S

Craftsmen tend to have an asocial nature. They have an inability to maintain close relationships. They look too cool, quiet, and independent. I suggest that they learn and apply social skills to get more involved with the social world.

Craftsmen have a weak ability to see the 'big picture'. They focus on the narrow scopes. They live in the here and now. They seldom set goals. I suggest that they set aside time to write down their goals and plan.

Craftsmen tend to work alone. They do not like others probing into their lives. They focus on being self-reliant. I suggest that they learn to embrace teamwork and that no one man is an island.

### FAMOUS EXAMPLES OF ISTP'S

- Robert Kiyosaki (Hawaiian Businessman)
- Angelina Jolie (American Actress)
- Rowan Atkinson (English Comedian)
- Stan Laurel (British Comic Actor)

## THE "ENFP" PSYCHOLOGIST

### OVERVIEW

The ENFp "psychologist" represents to me "the James T. Kirk" of the social world. He will take command of an organisation with zeal and optimism. He is ready to "go down with the ship", to stick with his teammates through good and bad times. He likes providing morale boosts to those under his command. He has a jovial nature.

Psychologists tend to go into business in something district-based such as a computer repair shop. They often cut corners without proper procedures in place. They tend to miss deadlines. However, they shun this under the carpets with their sensitive nature. This gets them out of trouble for poor business practices. In fact, they will take any "legal headaches" as part of the game of playing this weird thing we call business.

Psychologists are not inclined to build big businesses. This is due to the vast amounts of legal administration they perceive it would bring to them. They can and do commit to operating small businesses, which can run quite successfully for a while. It is common for them to get into business administration issues readily seeing the funny side of filing for bankruptcy. This is due to their ability to create a strong belief that it will all work out in the end.

Psychologists are on their guard and touchy by nature. They mostly act with doubt and mistrust towards the apparent motives of others. They readily report on government entities. They will investigate and condemn the rise of any 'New World Orders' that will enslave us all. They expect fraud and falseness from other people. Thus, they try to avoid all surprises by foreseeing their actions.

Psychologists tend to have a good sense of humour. They like to have a dash of irony and frivolousness. They show an acceptance of people in general.

## MODEL A: THE "ENFP" PSYCHOLOGIST

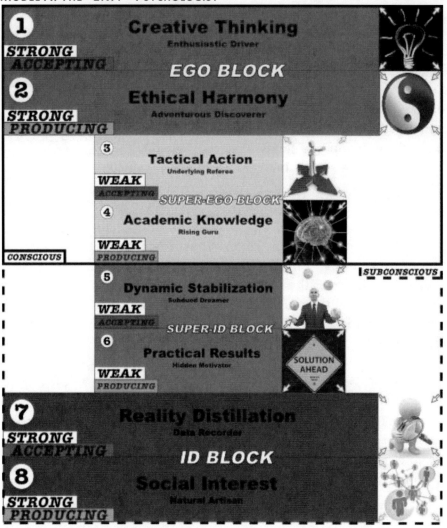

## ATTITUDE ANALYSIS: EGO BLOCK

### 1. ENTHUSIASTIC DRIVER - CREATIVE THINKING (CT)
*"...ALWAYS LOOKING FOR MORE MEANINGS..."*

Creative Thinking is the irrational first attitude. It leads the psychologist to live in a world of the unknown thriving with possibilities. Therefore, CT is like having a lens that reflects greater truths. He will like finding the 'big picture'.

Psychologists are always looking for more meanings in things. To deal with reality, he must account for the wider scope. For example, a strike in the public sector may be a reflection of a larger social issue. He needs to explore the broader context. This will change his perception of the whole by understanding its parts.

Hence, CT is a need to welcome the unknown always. It leads the psychologist to adjust to the unexpected. They have an approval of the hectic nature of the world.

## 2. Adventurous Discoverer - Ethical Harmony (EH)
### "...A strong sense of ethics..."

Ethical Harmony is the rational second attitude. It yields results of the CT attitude by adding a strong sense of ethics when dealing with people. The psychologist brings harmony to a place through their moral codes. For example, they may come out with sarcastic statements designed to harmonise relationships between people.

Hence, EH as the second mindset of the psychologist provides the morals in their affairs with others. For example, they may ensure harmony in the workplace.

## Attitude Analysis: Super-Ego Block

## 3. Underlying Referee - Tactical Action (TA)
### "...to enjoy life in the moment..."

Tactical Action is the third irrational attitude. It is one-half of the super-ego and conscience behind the stronger ego attitudes. For the psychologist, down-to-earth reactions to the world do not show on the surface much. They tend to have no concern for the past or future. For example, they like to accept people at face value.

Psychologists want to enjoy life in the moment. They may do this more than follow through on their grandiose visions of a better tomorrow for the local community. They do not like to enjoy life alone.

As a complex, the psychologist may become cross when their sense of enjoying life is threatened. He expects to enjoy life with a low regard to the costs. He does not want to get involved with reclusive people. Hence, TA as the third attitude leads the psychologist to take part in the surroundings. He takes great pleasure in an active community life.

## 4. RISING GURU - ACADEMIC KNOWLEDGE (AK)
### "...A WEAK SKILL FOR REFLECTION..."

Academic Knowledge is the fourth rational attitude. It is the second half of the super-ego and conscience behind the stronger ego attitudes. As the producing mindset of the TA attitude, this is a weak skill for reflection.

As a phobic mindset, this explains why psychologists tend to lack in-depth thoughts. They tend to have many fantastical ideas on society without a sound understanding of the issues. On the other hand, they require introspection to teach new subjects that take their interest.

Hence, AK is the timid mindset of the psychologist who does not want to go back to school so to speak. They will avoid philosophical debates if they can help it.

### ATTITUDE ANALYSIS: SUPER-ID BLOCK

## 5. SUBDUED DREAMER - DYNAMIC, STABILIZATION (DS)
### "...TO FIXATE ON THE KNOWN..."

Dynamic Stabilization is the fifth irrational attitude. It is one-half of the super-id, the conscience of the id. For the psychologist, this mindset is restless in anchoring them to the known. The conscious attitudes have sought upon the trends in the world. The DS attitude equates to the inner need to deal with a hectic reality. For example, in business, they may choose ideas that provide tried and tested results.

This swayable attitude may not ask for help in its private wish to concern them with the chaotic nature of the world. For example, after years of seeing trends, they may want to retire to a simple life.

Hence, DS is a dormant attitude that wants the psychologist to fixate on the known. A person with a strong conscious DS attitude can provoke a restart of this desire.

## 6. HIDDEN MOTIVATOR - PRACTICAL RESULTS (PR)
"...TO GET RESULTS..."

Practical Results is the sixth rational attitude. It is the second half of the super-id, the conscience of the id. For the psychologist, it yields results of the DS attitude by turning ideas into profits. This attitude does not work well in gaining results until helped by someone with PR as a conscious attitude.

As the hidden agenda of the psychologist, they may like to build wealth. This will assist them in turning dreams into reality. They may need help with this weak area of their subconscious mind.

Hence, PR is the weak attitude that wants to get results. For example, the psychologist needs to identify a trend and then, capitalise on it.

## ATTITUDE ANALYSIS: ID BLOCK

## 7. DATA RECORDER - REALITY DISTILLATION (RD)
"...TO NEGOTIATE WITH OTHERS..."

Reality Distillation is the seventh irrational attitude. It is one-half of the id, the most instinctual self. As we delve into the core of the psychologist's mind, we find concern for arguing through the extra details in reality. The RD mindset will fulfil itself under periods of stress or upset. For example, they could claim that people who work for a living are nothing more than pawns in a system.

Hence, RD is a strong subconscious mindset that provides the psychologist on a whim for negotiating with others. They may use these skills to stay focused and on-task.

## 8. NATURAL ARTISAN - SOCIAL INTEREST (SI)
"...AN AUTOMATIC ZEST FOR SOCIAL NETWORKING..."

Social Interest is the eighth rational attitude. It is the second half of the id, the most instinctual self. At the core of the psychologist's mind, we find an automatic zest for social networking. He may know all about equity and fairness. For example, he may be courteous in his dealings with others sharing surplus goods believing that others can make better use of them.

Hence, SI is the strong subconscious mindset that makes the psychologist a people person. This fuels his need to socialise often. He does not find it difficult to relate to others.

### PERSONAL DEVELOPMENT FOR ENFP'S

Psychologists tend to get the wrong idea about people. They have a somewhat paranoid and wary nature. This is due to their weak ability to understand people and phenomena to its fullest. I suggest that they take the time to learn about personality types and clarify their understanding of others.

Psychologists can make model conspiracy theorists. They see trends in the world that raise alarm bells in them. They do not like the idea of a 'big brother' society. I suggest that they tone down their sensitive perceptions to the world. This will enable them to get on with their lives without too much concern over 'secret society' movements.

Psychologists may get involved in half-baked businesses. They do not mind cutting corners. They may use their diplomatic skills to get them out of trouble with customers. I suggest that they learn to put into place proper business practices if they are to succeed in a big way.

### FAMOUS EXAMPLES OF ENFP'S
- Jason Statham (English Actor)
- Davina McCall (English TV Presenter)
- Uri Gellar (Israeli-British Performer)
- Cher Bono (American Singer-Songwriter)

# PART TWO: INTER-TYPE RELATIONS

*What makes a good interpersonal relationship?*

In Part One we looked at the complete Socion (the sixteen types). We looked at how they each function in the social world. In this Part Two, we will begin to analyse how personality types interact with each other based on the ordering of their psyche.

The theoretical model of the mind provided by the Model A leads to certain psychological assumptions about what constitutes a harmonious interpersonal relationship. Before we delve into the different inter-type relations, it will be helpful to understand these assumptions. This will allow you to comprehend better why some relations are better/worse than others.

The following assumptions of the Model A explains why interpersonal relationships can be so challenging:

1. Each information element represents to me the perception of a different facet of reality.
2. Each type has a different ordering of the information elements thus a different perception of reality (or attitudes).
3. The division of the psyche into the conscious and subconscious results in people being unaware of their unconscious attitudes.
4. Each type has weak and strong attitudes which affect their judgments and motivations.

This leads me to the conclusion that from an information processing standpoint each type is "incomplete" in the sense that they have weak and subconscious attitudes. Therefore, in inter-type relations, they ideally want relationships that strengthen their weak attitudes.

From this model of the psyche the optimal psychological relationship between two types occurs when all the following conditions are true:

- Information elements that are accepting in one type must be accepting in the other type;
- Information elements that are producing in one type must be producing in the other type;

- Information elements that are conscious of one type must be subconscious of the other type;
- Information elements that are weak of one type must be strong in the other type;

The most optimal inter-type relation that meets all the above criteria is the "duality" relationship. This serves as the benchmark by which all other inter-type relationships are compared.

**Please Note: Although "duality" is optimal from a Socionics perspective we have to understand what that means. It just means from an information processing standpoint that it is the most psychologically harmonious relation. However, since each person varies in their socialisation, attitudes and level of character development it is not a guarantee of peaceful relations on a personal level.**

I will explain duality later in this part of the book but as you can see in the following diagram why the INTj's dual is the ESFj based on the ordering of their information elements. All other inter-type relations are defined based on their variance from duality.

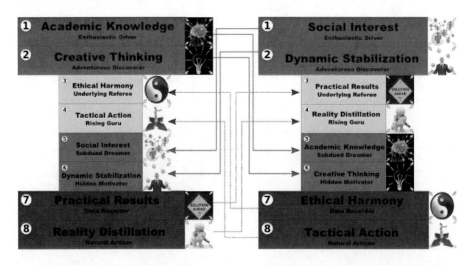

In each inter-type relations diagram, I will use arrowheads to denote when accepting or producing attitudes of one type corresponds directly with another accepting or producing attitude respectively of another type. Conversely, I will use semi-circles as the head to denote when an accepting attitude corresponds with a producing attitude and vice-versa.

It is beyond the scope of this book to detail the relations for each and every type regarding the remaining types that they are associated with. For illustrative purposes, I have picked The "INTj" Analyst as the primary type to compare against other types. As you read on you will find special merged versions of the Model A that juxtaposes the analyst with its corresponding types. At the end of this overview, you will find a chart that will allow you to determine your intertype relations.

Remember to take careful notice of the difference in the position of the eight information elements as this represents the "structural view" of how types differ. It also offers a clue as to how each inter-type relationship got named. For example, relations of supervision will clearly show how one type dominates the other due to the relative positioning of a particular attitude thus illustrating this asymmetric relationship.

In a proceeding chapter we will take a look at the "inner-quadra symmetric relations", that is, the interactions of personality types that reside inside the same Quadra. As previously discussed a Quadra is a structural unit of the Socion. It is also the chief "small group" by which we place types together that share common values, motivations, and the same standing in the social hierarchy. By default, members of the same Quadra usually enjoy the most comfortable relationships.

Later on, we will take a look at the "outer-quadra symmetric relations", that is, the interactions of personality types that a) reside outside the same Quadra, and b) have zero difference on the social hierarchy. As the name suggests, these relations can have all sorts of compatibility issues ranging from suspicion to misunderstanding, etc. However, since no one inter-type relationship is classified as 'the best', they all have their potential uses. For example, to achieve a healthy group with outer-quadra types usually, requires an appreciation of the default social dynamics.

Lastly, we will take a look at the "outer-quadra asymmetric relations", that is, the interactions of personality types that a) reside outside the same Quadra, and b) have some difference on the social hierarchy. The off-balanced hierarchical nature of these relations means that one type is always in a more favourable position than the other. This results in two subtypes of asymmetric relation: supervision (power struggle) and benefaction (unequal respect).

# INTER-TYPE RELATIONS CHART

The following chart shows a complete matrix of the sixteen types compared to their corresponding types. The grey shaded areas represent the "inner quadra relations", the blank white areas represent the "outer quadra relations", and the diagonally striped areas represent the "asymmetric relations".

| | INTj | ESFj | ISFp | ENTp | ISTj | ENFj | INFp | ESTp | ISFj | ENTj | INTp | ESFp | INFj | ESTj | ISTp | ENFp |
|---|---|---|---|---|---|---|---|---|---|---|---|---|---|---|---|---|
| INTj | Id | Dl | Ac | Mr | Ki | Pd | B▲ | S▲ | Se | Ex | Qi | Co | Bu | Mg | B▼ | S▼ |
| ESFj | Dl | Id | Mr | Ac | Pd | Ki | S▲ | B▲ | Ex | Se | Co | Qi | Mg | Bu | S▼ | B▼ |
| ISFp | Ac | Mr | Id | Dl | B▼ | S▼ | Bu | Mg | Qi | Co | Se | Ex | B▲ | S▲ | Ki | Pd |
| ENTp | Mr | Ac | Dl | Id | S▼ | B▼ | Mg | Bu | Co | Qi | Ex | Se | S▲ | B▲ | Pd | Ki |
| ISTj | Ki | Pd | B▲ | S▲ | Id | Dl | Ac | Mr | Bu | Mg | B▼ | S▼ | Se | Ex | Qi | Co |
| ENFj | Pd | Ki | S▲ | B▲ | Dl | Id | Mr | Ac | Mg | Bu | S▼ | B▼ | Ex | Se | Co | Qi |
| INFp | B▼ | S▼ | Bu | Mg | Ac | Mr | Id | Dl | B▲ | S▲ | Ki | Pd | Qi | Co | Se | Ex |
| ESTp | S▼ | B▼ | Mg | Bu | Mr | Ac | Dl | Id | S▲ | B▲ | Pd | Ki | Co | Qi | Ex | Se |
| ISFj | Se | Ex | Qi | Co | Bu | Mg | B▼ | S▼ | Id | Dl | Ac | Mr | Ki | Pd | B▲ | S▲ |
| ENTj | Ex | Se | Co | Qi | Mg | Bu | S▼ | B▼ | Dl | Id | Mr | Ac | Pd | Ki | S▲ | B▲ |
| INTp | Qi | Co | Se | Ex | B▲ | S▲ | Ki | Pd | Ac | Mr | Id | Dl | B▼ | S▼ | Bu | Mg |
| ESFp | Co | Qi | Ex | Se | S▲ | B▲ | Pd | Ki | Mr | Ac | Dl | Id | S▼ | B▼ | Mg | Bu |
| INFj | Bu | Mg | B▼ | S▼ | Se | Ex | Qi | Co | Ki | Pd | B▲ | S▲ | Id | Dl | Ac | Mr |
| ESTj | Mg | Bu | S▼ | B▼ | Ex | Se | Co | Qi | Pd | Ki | S▲ | B▲ | Dl | Id | Mr | Ac |
| ISTp | B▲ | S▲ | Ki | Pd | Qi | Co | Se | Ex | B▼ | S▼ | Bu | Mg | Ac | Mr | Id | Dl |
| ENFp | S▲ | B▲ | Pd | Ki | Co | Qi | Ex | Se | S▼ | B▼ | Mg | Bu | Mr | Ac | Dl | Id |

### Inner-Quadra Relations

(Id) Identity; (Mr) Mirror; (Ac) Activity; (Dl) Duality

### Outer-Quadra Relations

(Ki) Kindred; (Pd) Partial-Duality; (Ex) Extinguishment; (Se) Super-ego;

(Bu) Business; (Mg) Mirage; (Qi) Quasi-Identity; (Co) Conflicting

### Asymmetric Relations

Where the Types in the **Top Columns** precede the **Left Columns** as either…

(S▲) Supervisor, (S▼) Supervisee, (B▲) Benefactor or (B▼) Beneficiary

E.g. An ESFj is Supervisor to an ISTp; An INTp is Beneficiary to an ISTj etc.

# INNER-QUADRA SYMMETRIC RELATIONS

## DUALITY RELATIONS
## "YIN AND YANG"

## AT A GLANCE
Duality relations offer the opportunity for partners to "be themselves" and are usually conflict-free.

It is Hetroverted meaning that the relationship consists of one introverted and one extroverted type.

It is Symmetrical meaning that partners affect each other equally.

It is also Energy Based meaning that the conscious attitudes of one partner "talks" to the subconscious attitudes of the other. This has a major subconscious impact since the exchange of information is attractive by nature.

Finally, a Small Psychological Distance is fostered whereby the relationship consists of two rational (j) or two irrational (p) types whom, for the most part, lock into the same rhythm.

An example of duality relations, comparing one INTj – Analyst with one ESFj – Enthusiast.

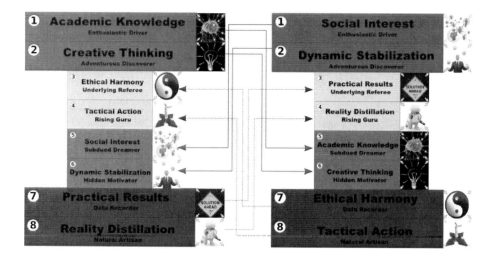

**Comments:**
- The conscious attitudes of one partner are the same as the subconscious attitudes of the other.
- "Complementary Attitudes" where each partner provides what the other needs automatically.
- Promotes self-actualization in both partners.

As we can see from the table above, the strong ego block of both partners "talks" to the weak super-id block of the other. Similar to activity relations, one partner can communicate with the super-id child-like conscience of the other.

The Natural Artisan attitude is instinctual and automatically creates for yourself and others. Since the strong id blocks are in sync with the other dual's weak super-ego – your weak points are instinctively protected and thus you can 'be yourself' without any pressure to change yourself to relate. Any inferiority complexes are relaxed.

The relationship is energy based making it attractive for both partners. Duals can usually talk about anything without fear of being misunderstood. They can reach moments of silence where simply being in each other's company is calming and desirable. Since duals have little or nothing to prove to each other, they can eventually become entirely inter-dependent using their spare energies for their own endeavours.

Due to the conscious and subconscious complementary nature of the information elements, one might say that their "dual" is the type of their dreams. Therefore a dual partner will accept you for what you are and if there is such a thing as "true love" or "true friendship" then it would probably have the best chances to develop in a duality relation. I know of many harmonious dual couples that have lasted in relationships for years.

Each partner of a duality relation can seem like a complementary half of a complete unit. They share a self-actualizing balance between introversion and extroversion, ethics and logic, sensory and intuition.

Duals help each other achieve psychological balance. You are bound to notice the inherent harmony and organic naturalness of this relation type. The cliché that there is always plenty more fish in the sea perhaps takes on a new meaning when we expand on it to say that statistically there are many potential relationships to be formed. With the identification of the duality relation, I would optimistically conclude that everyone has not one but several potential "soul mates" in existence.

I believe that Carl Jung was accurate when he concluded that "the meeting of two personalities is like the contact of two chemical substances: if there is any reaction, both are transformed". In other words, while duality relations have a greater likelihood of being harmonious it is not a guarantee of a healthy relationship. Other factors come into play, and it should be remembered that there are numerous people one can have a duality relation with. That being said, it can be difficult to notice a potential dual and even easier to pass by as not worthy of your attention.

In conclusion, duality relations can provide emotional equilibrium freeing each from any manifested neuroses and phobias about their attitudes and society. Theoretically, it is the most favourable relationship although potentially the hardest to find and develop due to many variables that could affect its introduction. One partner may feel the other is "out of their league" while the other may only believe that the other partner is not worthy of their attention, at first. However, long term duality relations tend to become quite unbreakable hence it is likely to conclude that duals who meet in early childhood (unknowingly of course) usually end up together for a very long time, perhaps for a lifetime.

## ACTIVITY RELATIONS
## "EXPECT A REACTION."

## AT A GLANCE
Activity relations are stimulating, also being the easiest and quickest to start.

It is Monoverted meaning that the relationship consists of two introverted or two extroverted types.

It is Symmetrical meaning that partners affect each other equally.

It is also Energy Based meaning that the conscious attitudes of one partner "talks" to the subconscious attitudes of the other. This has a major subconscious impact since the exchange of information is attractive by nature.

Finally, a Large Psychological Distance is fostered whereby the relationship consists of one rational (j) and one irrational (p) type whom, for the most part, have different rhythms, different moods, and different reactions in the same situation.

An example of activity relations, comparing one INTj – Analyst with one ISFp – Mediator.

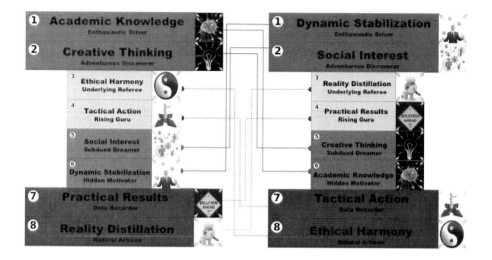

**Comments:**

- The conscious Enthusiastic Driver attitude of both partners is the Hidden Motivator attitude of the other.
- The conscious Adventurous Discover attitude of both partners is the Subdued Dreamer attitude of the other.
- All conscious attitudes of both partners are found in the subconscious area of the other.
- Similar to Duality relations except that accepting attitudes correspond with producing attitudes and vice-versa.

As we can see from the table above, the strong ego block of both partners "talks" to the weak super-id block of the other thus making these relations the easiest and quickest to start. In essence, information metabolised into the super-id could be viewed as refreshing and stimulating by this child-like conscience. For example, I have known mediators to be receptive to the INTj's strong noticing of external possibilities (CT) and highly individualised understandings (AK) and conversely the INTj has been receptive to their strong perspective on socially relating in the world (SI) and considering known processes (DS).

The relationship is energy based thus making it attractive for both partners. However since activity relations are arrhythmic, this may be a reason why partners experience minor misunderstandings from time to time. Therefore the relationship is one of oscillation ranging from an expected stimulation mentally and physically to over-stimulation where both partners need to recover before another cycle of activity.

In conclusion, activity relations are attractive and ideal for leisure.

## Mirror Relations
## "A constructive critic."

## AT A GLANCE

Mirror relations offer a harmonious and mutually corrective relationship.

It is Hetroverted meaning that the relationship consists of one introverted and one extroverted type.

It is Symmetrical meaning that partners affect each other equally.

It is also Information Based meaning that the conscious attitudes of one partner "talks" to the conscious attitudes of the other. This has a minor subconscious impact since the exchange of information is repulsive by nature.

Finally, a Large Psychological Distance is fostered whereby the relationship consists of one rational (j) and one irrational (p) type whom, for the most part, have different rhythms, different moods, and different reactions in the same situation.

An example of mirror relations, comparing one INTj – Analyst with an ENTp – Searcher.

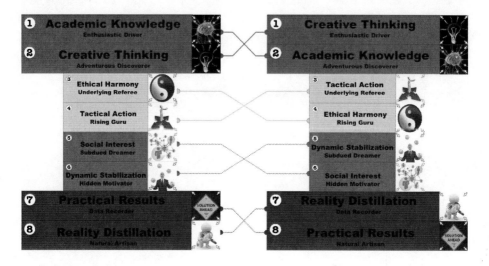

**Comments:**

- Each attitude block is reversed.
- All conscious attitudes exist within the same conscious area for both partners.
- All subconscious attitudes exist within the same subconscious area for both partners.

As we can see from the table above, the accepting (odd) attitudes of one partner are the producing (even) attitudes of the other. Since each block of the psyche contains the same attitudes (in reverse order) these partners usually realise that they are very like-minded with similar interests and ideas.

The reason that this relationship is mutually corrective is that a more confident producing attitude from a partner can "talk" to a similar accepting attitude of the other. For example, in the ego block, the Analyst has a primary strength of revealing the internal structure of things, knowledge which he may share with the Searcher, who may find his thinking interesting and even create a new understanding as a result since AK is his Adventurous Discover attitude.

This usually results in either constructive feedback that is appreciated as useful or a hot dispute to prove their opinions.

From experience, mirror partners tend to be good friends due to similar psyches and having a slightly different understanding of the same problems which aids in mutual corrections for both. For example, a Searcher with an Underlying Referee attitude of TA may suggest ways the Analyst with his weak TA could enjoy life more while conversely, the Analyst with his Underlying Referee attitude of EH may suggest what is ethically correct in a given situation to the weak EH of the Searcher.

The relationship is information based and as such will unlikely to be arousing since attitudes don't "talk" to the subconscious. Mirror relations are arrhythmic i.e. have a significant psychological distance which is likely to be one of the primary sources of discomfort. For example, where the rational (j) partner may prefer to know what is happening next in a given situation the irrational (p) partner may be more spontaneous and adaptable thus creating this vast psychological distance. This situation typically changes in the presence of a third person within the same Quadra who is a Dual to one partner and thus an Activity partner to the other.

In conclusion, mirror relations are, in a nutshell, mutually handy to have.

## IDENTITY RELATIONS
### "SEPARATED AT BIRTH PERHAPS?"

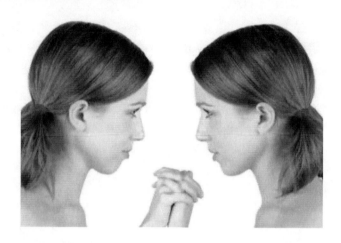

## AT A GLANCE

Identity relations offer complete understanding and the opportunity for self-development.

It is Monoverted meaning that the relationship consists of two introverted or two extroverted types.

It is Symmetrical meaning that partners affect each other equally.

It is also Information Based meaning that the conscious attitudes of one partner "talks" to the conscious attitudes of the other. This has a minor subconscious impact since the exchange of information is repulsive by nature.

Finally, a Small Psychological Distance is fostered whereby the relationship consists of two rational (j) or two irrational (p) types whom, for the most part, lock into the same rhythm.

An example of identical relations, comparing two INTj – Analysts.

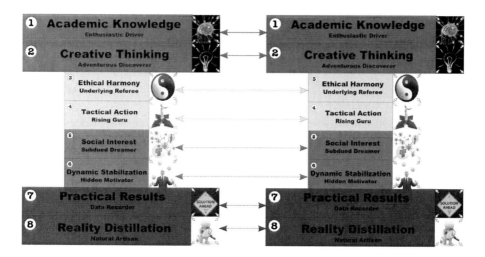

## Comments:

- All attitudes are identically positioned where accepting and producing attitudes correspond with each other correctly.
- No conscious to the subconscious impact of the attitudes between partners.

As we can see from the table above, both partners have identical psychological structures. However, as two distinct individuals in society with varying life experiences and upbringings they would both be unique in their right.

These relations exist between each of the sixteen psychological types e.g. INTj with INTj, ESFj with ESFj, etc. Since individuals are of the same type, there is usually a complete understanding between partners though often an inability to help each other.

Identity relations have the same attitude ordering of the psyche between partners and may appear to have similar understandings, conclusions and problems with the world which may be more or less dealt with as individuals.

Thus they would likely feel great empathy towards their identity partner whom they identify with. Each identity partner may have possessed varying life wisdom. It usually results in the formation of a mentoring relationship with each sharing their differences in real world experience and personal knowledge. For example, the partner perceived as being on a higher level in personal development offers advice to the identity partner in the hope that it may help get them through a problem already faced.

For the sustainment of identity relations, one partner takes on the role of a dual forming a quasi "duality relation" (discussed previously). This usually occurs in this monoverted relationship automatically where each type subconsciously tries to compensate for the information elements lacking consciously. For example, one analyst may act like a quasi-enthusiast thereby taking care of the extroverted and emotional aspects usually found in this particular (quasi-) duality relationship.

However, since the information exchange is repulsive i.e. information based, it may be difficult for a partner to integrate or be motivated into action by such interactions since there is little or no arousal of the subconscious. Identity relations are more likely to 'plant seeds' rather than invoke rapid learning, action and growth. There is only so much one can learn from their identity relation at any one time. When partners have expended their energy exchanging information, the relationships can become quite neutral.

In conclusion, identity relations promote self-development between partners where possible solutions to common problems can be reviewed from the perspective of like-minded philosophy. It is analogous to an alternative self from a parallel universe showing you what they accomplished given the same set of psychological attitudes. Each developed their character from the unique challenges and different worldly circumstances they encountered. Therefore identity partners can be secretively envious of each other as they try to fit the same social niche i.e. having similar potential skill sets that compete for attention.

# OUTER-QUADRA SYMMETRIC RELATIONS

## KINDRED RELATIONS
### "ARE WE NOT RELATED?"

## AT A GLANCE
The partners in kindred relations appear deceptively similar. Both partners remain unreceptive to each other's advice. This is due to no subconscious influence on each other as they have the same information elements in both their subconscious and conscious blocks. What differs from a structural viewpoint is the ordering of the information elements in each block.

It is Monoverted meaning that the relationship consists of two introverted or two extroverted types.

It is Symmetrical meaning that partners affect each other equally.

It is also Information Based meaning that the conscious attitudes of one partner "talks" to the conscious attitudes of the other. This has a minor subconscious impact since the exchange of information is repulsive by nature.

Finally, a Small Psychological Distance is fostered whereby the relationship consists of two rational (j) or two irrational (p) types whom, for the most part, lock into the same rhythm.

An example of kindred relations, comparing one INTj – Analyst with one ISTj – Inspector.

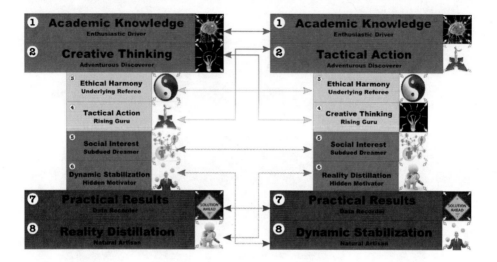

**Comments:**

- All conscious attitudes exist within the same conscious area for both partners.
- All subconscious attitudes exist within the same subconscious area for both partners.
- Attitudes 2 and 4 are reversed as well as 6 and 8.

If we glanced at the table above, we might notice obvious similarities between kindred partners. All the accepting attitudes are identical while all the producing attitudes are reversed. Kindred partners appear deceptively similar. Both types perceive their worlds similarly as their accepting attitudes are in the same position. Their variance is due to the different ordering of their producing attitudes which results in various interests.

The relationship is information based which makes it repulsive to both partners. One benefit of kindred relations is the refining of one's social skills. This is because partners have many similarities yet sufficiently different attitudes for the relationship to be interesting. However, all relations of this type tend to become boring and stagnant over time though may be perceived as beneficial and dynamic initially. In other words, there is a little or no energy alluring us back to our kindred partners. Another problem with these relationships is that the partners are unreceptive to information exchanged. Therefore, it is common for one partner to offer advice that remains useful for himself and unheeded by the other. While it may seem nice to discuss local or world-views, both partners usually find the difference of opinions to be incompatible and seldom reach an agreement especially when offering personal advice.

In conclusion, kindred relations usually develop into unexciting, stagnating and unproductive interactions.

## PARTIAL-DUALITY RELATIONS
### "SO CLOSE YET SO FAR."

## AT A GLANCE
Partial-Duality relations provide an incomplete duality relationship leading to unintentional quarrels.

It is Hetroverted meaning that the relationship consists of one introverted and one extroverted type.

It is Symmetrical meaning that partners affect each other equally.

It is also Energy Based meaning that the conscious attitudes of one partner "talks" to the subconscious attitudes of the other. This has a major subconscious impact since the exchange of information is attractive by nature.

Finally, a Small Psychological Distance is fostered whereby the relationship consists of two rational (j) or two irrational (p) types whom, for the most part, lock into the same rhythm.

An example of partial-duality relations, comparing one INTj – Analyst with one ENFj – Actor.

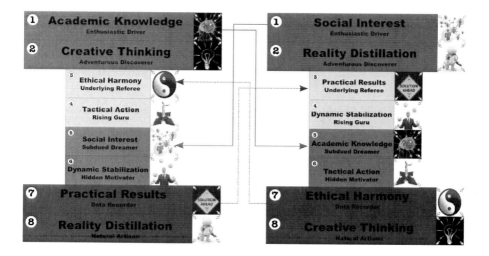

## Comments:

- All conscious attitudes of both partners are found in the subconscious area of the other.
- The conscious Enthusiastic Driver attitude of both partners is the Subdued Dreamer attitude of the other.
- The subconscious Data Recorder attitude of both partners is the Underlying Referee attitude of the other.
- Only two strong (out of four) attitudes complement two weak (out of four) attitudes in each partner are making this duality incomplete.

As we can see from the table above, the strong Enthusiastic Driver attitude of both partners "talks" to the weak Subdued Dreamer attitude - child-like conscience of the other partner.

At first glance, it may appear these relationships provide for each other's psychological needs like a duality relationship would. However, the underlying reality is that complete duality is unachievable. This is due to only one of the conscious attitudes helping the other partner's weak subconscious attitudes. The remaining attitudes cannot help since they share the same relative strengths.

The relationship is energy based making it attractive for both partners. Similar to a duality relation, partners can discuss many topics and from an outsider's perspective, the relationship can seem passionate and loving.

The reality is that a lot of conscious effort is required to make things work since only one strong conscious attitude of each partner supports a weak subconscious of the other.

In conclusion, partial-duality relations result in a fluctuating relationship with many contrasts of elation and sadness towards each other.

EXTINGUISHING RELATIONS
"WARNING: ATTITUDES MAY BE FLAMMABLE."

## AT A GLANCE

Extinguishing relations ends up with an unstable psychological distance and can become suspicious over time.

It is Hetroverted meaning that the relationship consists of one introverted and one extroverted type.

It is Symmetrical meaning that partners affect each other equally.

It is also Energy Based meaning that the conscious attitudes of one partner "talks" to the subconscious attitudes of the other. This has a major subconscious impact since the exchange of information is attractive by nature.

Finally, a Small Psychological Distance is fostered whereby the relationship consists of two rational (j) or two irrational (p) types whom, for the most part, lock into the same rhythm.

An example of extinguishing relations, comparing one INTj – Analyst with one ENTj – Pioneer.

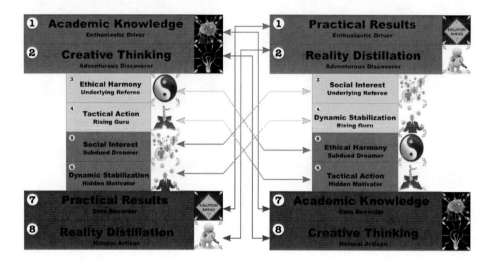

**Comments:**

- All conscious attitudes of both partners are found in the subconscious area of the other.
- In each position, where one type has the introverted version of an information element the other type has the corresponding extroverted version and vice versa. For example, where one type has Creative Thinking (extroverted), the other type has Reality Distillation (introverted).
- No strong attitudes correspond to any weak attitudes and vice versa.

As we can see from the table above, each attitude is the same for both partners albeit with a reversal of orientation. Extinguishing relations are energy based meaning that partners can expect to be drawn to each other. The ordering of their psyches is similar though inverted so they tend to have similar interests. However, their varying perceptions of the world cause them to look at reality differently. This leads to a situation where both parties cannot comprehend each other's viewpoints.

In this relationship, both partners activate each other subconsciously but have different outlooks. Consequently, both parties usually become frustrated and unsuccessful in their attempts to build rapport. Thus there is an inability to form a harmonious and stable relationship as each person's strength opposes the other. It is usually the case that the introverted partner becomes wary and detached as they continue the interaction. The extroverted partner tends to take a highly skeptical view of the relationship as a whole based on the behaviour of the introverted partner. This continued miscommunication increases as the relationship progresses.

In conclusion, extinguishing relations have an unstable psychological distance as a result of similar interests but divergent perspectives.

## SUPER-EGO RELATIONS
## "DECEPTIVE ADMIRATION."

## AT A GLANCE
Super-Ego relations tend to display mutual respect between partners though ends up egotistical.

It is Monoverted meaning that the relationship consists of two introverted or two extroverted types.

It is Symmetrical meaning that partners affect each other equally.

It is also Information Based meaning that the conscious attitudes of one partner "talks" to the conscious attitudes of the other. This has a minor subconscious impact since the exchange of information is repulsive by nature.

Finally, a Small Psychological Distance is fostered whereby the relationship consists of two rational (j) or two irrational (p) types whom, for the most part, lock into the same rhythm.

An example of super-ego relations, comparing one INTj – Analyst with one ISFj – Guardian.

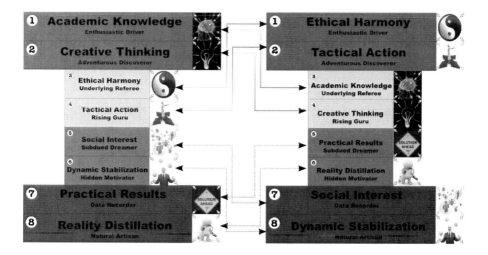

**Comments:**

- Both partners have the same attitudes within their conscious areas.
- Both partners have the same attitudes within their subconscious areas.
- Attitude 1 and 3, 2 and 4, 5 and 7, 6 and 8 are reversed.
- All weak attitudes are influenced in some way by the similar strong attitudes in the other partner, in respective conscious and subconscious blocks.

As we can see from the table above, the ego block of each partner corresponds with the superego block of the other. In reality, this usually manifests as advice spoken between the strong ego of each partner and their weak superego conscience.

For example, an INTj could learn meticulously how to program a video recorder and teach this knowledge to his Super-Ego relation (ISFj). Since the strong attitudes of the INTj's ego are the weak attitudes of the ISFj's super-ego, there is a slight hindrance in the way these elements interact. In other words, the strong ego attitudes of one partner "talking" to the weak super-ego attitudes of the other are like a parent explaining something to a young child. This results in frustration between both partners although when committed and receptive towards one another, results can be achieved. The frustration comes from each partner's ego excessively trying to explain things to the other person's super-ego.

In conclusion, superego relations are usually one of mutual respect. While not attractive as such, they can be a good mix of learning. When information exchange becomes wearisome, it wouldn't be uncommon to expect arguments just for the sake of venting any frustrations. For example, it is analogous to a member of the current generation appreciating something that a member of the previous generation does not. Consequently, both may find it frustrating to understand where each is coming from as they try to explain any cultural differences.

## Business Relations
### "Superficial cooperation."

## AT A GLANCE

Business relations offer real understanding and empathy towards similar problems.

It is Monoverted meaning that the relationship consists of two introverted or two extroverted types.

It is Symmetrical meaning that partners affect each other equally.

It is also Information Based meaning that the conscious attitudes of one partner "talks" to the conscious attitudes of the other. This has a minor subconscious impact since the exchange of information is repulsive by nature.

Finally, a Small Psychological Distance is fostered whereby the relationship consists of two rational (j) or two irrational (p) types whom, for the most part, lock into the same rhythm.

An example of business relations, comparing one INTj – Analyst with one INFj – Humanist.

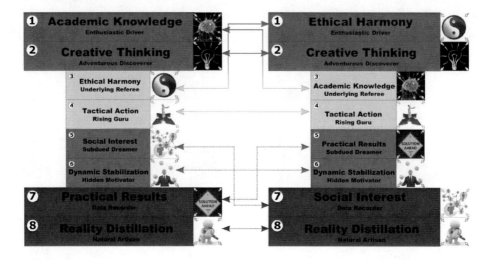

**Comments:**

- Both partners have the same attitudes within their conscious areas.
- Both partners have the same attitudes within their subconscious areas.
- Odd-numbered attitudes 1 and 3, 5 and 7 are reversed.
- Even-numbered attitudes 2 and 4, 6 and 8 are identical.

As we can see from the table above, the symbols of the attitudes seem almost identical in appearance and placement. Partners in this relationship are very similar notably sharing the same Rising Guru attitude (shyness). Since this is the case partners can naturally empathise with each other's weaknesses thus there is a good understanding of this relationship.

These relations are information based and as such are repulsive with regards to information exchange. Partners strengths are half incompatible and don't provide exactly what the other partner wants though there is usually an average degree of comfort since there is little to fight over.

In conclusion, business relations are one of acquaintance, which in my experience often come together literally in matters of collaborating courses of action in life and work issues.

## MIRAGE RELATIONS
## "CAN SHADOWS RELATE?"

## AT A GLANCE

Mirage relations tend to have a growing laziness about them while fostering a deceptive like-mindedness.

Mirage relations are Hetroverted meaning that the relationship consists of one introverted and one extroverted type.

It is Symmetrical meaning that partners affect each other equally.

It is also Energy Based meaning that the conscious attitudes of one partner "talks" to the subconscious attitudes of the other with minor conscious impact thus the exchange of information is attractive by nature.

Finally, a Small Psychological Distance is fostered whereby the relationship consists of two rational (j) or two irrational (p) types whom, for the most part, lock into the same rhythm.

An example of mirage relations, comparing one INTj – Analyst with one ESTj – Director.

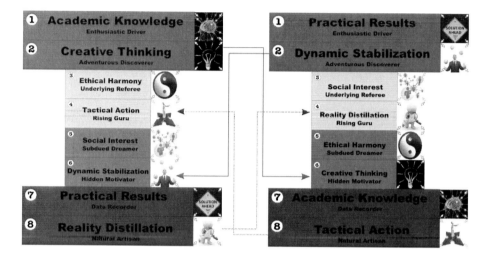

**Comments:**

- All conscious attitudes of both partners are found in the subconscious area of the other.
- The Adventurous Discoverer attitude of both partners is the Hidden Motivator attitude of the other.

As we can see from the table above, this relationship is quasi-identical to extinguishment relations where the odd functions are the same except for their orientations or focus.

It could just be a superficial observation although an important one because it leads me to conclude that there is a distinct difference and similarity.

Apparently, these relations are of growing laziness, and I can agree with that. It is energy based and thus attractive, information exchange between partners can be quite relaxing and receptive. However, it can take much effort to understand each other's intentions which may get in the way of achieving goals.

Since each partner's Adventurous Discoverer attitude stimulates or arouses the Hidden Motivator attitude of the other, this would be the likely reason for the attraction. As discussed previously, the naïve Hidden Motivator attitude likes and needs to be helped and praised.

In conclusion, mirage relations are attractive, partly stimulating and thus somewhat handy in a pseudo-practical kind of way.

## QUASI-IDENTITY RELATIONS
## "REVERSE PSYCHOLOGY."

## AT A GLANCE
Quasi-Identical relations have major misunderstandings while remaining relatively peaceful.

It is Monoverted meaning that the relationship consists of two introverted or two extroverted types.

It is Symmetrical meaning that partners affect each other equally.

It is also Energy Based meaning that the conscious attitudes of one partner "talks" to the subconscious attitudes of the other. This has a major subconscious impact since the exchange of information is attractive by nature.

Finally, a Large Psychological Distance is fostered whereby the relationship consists of one rational (j) and one irrational (p) type whom, for the most part, have different rhythms, different moods, and different reactions in the same situation.

An example of quasi-identity relations, comparing one INTj – Analyst with one INTp – Critic.

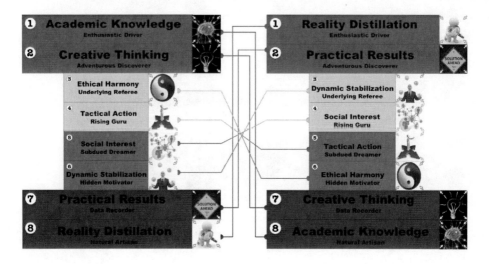

**Comments:**
- All conscious attitudes of both partners are found in the subconscious area of the other.
- Attitudes 1 to 8 for both partners equal attitudes 8 to 1 for the other.
- Accepting attitudes correspond with producing attitudes and vice-versa.

As we can see from the table above, the overall ordering of the psyche is inverted. I like to use an analogy that quasi-identity partners are from alternate universes whose demeanour and personal paradigms are logically misunderstood, in essence, where the rules of one universe are upside-down about the other.

So, if your quasi-identity partner decides to write a novel, it may have to go through some upside-down translation matrix in the other partner's mind before it can be understood. Interestingly, these relations are energy based making them attractive.

In this relation, we have two types from different Quadras. Given the inverted ordering of their psyches, their same attitudes have the same strength but different order. As a result of this, they tend to have similar interests but different perspectives on subjects. Also, since their attitudes have the same relative strength, they notice the same facets of reality but articulate and deal with them differently.

Since one type's Enthusiastic Driver is the other's Natural Artisan they tend to admire each other's skilful use of their first attitude. The flip side of this is that they tend to want to correct each other's approach to a situation as the inverted nature of their psyches puts a different perspective on reality.

Each has the same weak attitudes albeit in different positions. This causes them to empathise with each other, but they are unable to meet each other's psychological needs. The combination of the different perspectives and inability to speak to each other's weak attitudes can lead to a sense of under-appreciation, misunderstanding and irritation with each other. These relations can end up with a feeling of disappointment as the partners tend to drain each other whereby weak attitudes don't get taken care of. However, if the relationship is based on mutual interests it can be harmonious albeit partners will have to seek other avenues to meet their psychological needs.

In conclusion, quasi-identity relations are intellectually stimulating, relatively peaceful despite any perceived misunderstandings while not providing what each partner psychologically needs. Both partners need to realise that solutions that work for themselves will not necessarily meet the needs of the other. With mutual understanding, this relation can provide results since they can bring a different perspective to the same situation or challenge.

## CONFLICTING RELATIONS
## "DON'T ROCK MY BOAT."

## AT A GLANCE
Conflicting relationships display increasing contentiousness with poor regard for each partner's weak attitudes.

It is Hetroverted meaning that the relationship consists of one introverted and one extroverted type.

It is Symmetrical meaning that partners affect each other equally.

It is also Information Based meaning that the conscious attitudes of one partner "talks" to the conscious attitudes of the other. This has a minor subconscious impact since the exchange of information is repulsive by nature.

Finally, a Large Psychological Distance is fostered whereby the relationship consists of one rational (j) and one irrational (p) type whom, for the most part, have different rhythms, different moods, and different reactions in the same situation.

An example of conflicting relations, comparing one INTj – Analyst with one ESFp – Ambassador.

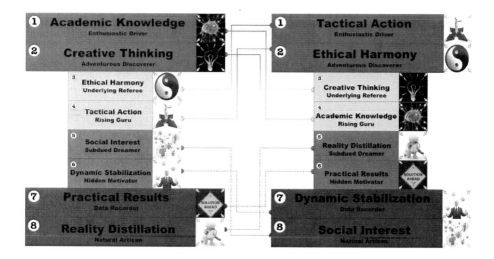

**Comments:**

- All conscious attitudes exist within the same conscious area for both partners.
- All subconscious attitudes exist within the same subconscious area for both partners.
- Attitudes 1 to 4 for both partners equal attitude 4 to 1 for the other.
- Attitudes 5 to 8 for both partners equal attitudes 8 to 5 for the other.
- The Enthusiastic Driver attitude of both partners is the Rising Guru attitude (shyness) of the other.
- Accepting attitudes correspond with producing attitudes and vice-versa.

As we can see from the table above, each corresponding block of the psyche contains unique and differing attitudes. To all intents and purposes, partners are complete opposites.

In these relations, each partner communicates a significant amount of information from their strong, accepting attitudes to the weak producing attitudes of the other. However, this is all done within the same conscious or subconscious blocks where each partner is unable to digest this information leaving them both disorganised and overwhelmed.

As you notice from our example of the INTj and ESFp they, differ on all basic dichotomies. The difference in rhythm i.e. where one partner is rational and the other is irrational causes further awkwardness as these relations advance.

While conflicting partners may appreciate each other's strengths, they soon become conscious of the intrinsic differences in their motivations, attitudes and perspectives. Given that they have no similarities in their attitudes this type of relationship can only be maintained from a long psychological distance. However, any close interpersonal interaction results in miscommunication and disagreeableness. The resulting conflict tends to see both partners entrenched in their position since they cannot understand each other's perspectives. Since they tend to overwhelm each other's weak attitudes, this leads to suspicion of each person's intentions. The strength of one partner's ego is the vulnerability of the other partner's superego which means that for the most part there is a disregard and understanding towards each other's apparent weaknesses. Consequently, we have two types of usually no common interests or understanding of each other's outlooks. This makes any collaboration tough.

It is a commonly held belief that "opposites attract" though since this relationship is information based, it is fact repulsive by nature. For example, an ESFp, a more here-and-now type, would likely be living a more hedonistic lifestyle when compared to the INTj, a more future-thinking type probably orientating to a more ascetic lifestyle.

In conclusion, in conflicting relations, there is always a potential for an explosive reaction. This is because each partner tries to express themselves in ways that the other partner is seldom familiar or strong in.

# OUTER-QUADRA ASYMMETRIC RELATIONS

## RELATIONS OF SUPERVISION
## "YOUR WEAKNESS IS MY STRENGTH."

## AT A GLANCE

Relations of Supervision involve two aspects where the Supervisor shows authority over the Shyness of the Supervisee, and the Supervisee is the 'object of attention' in the presence of the Supervisor.

It is Hetroverted meaning that the relationship consists of one introverted and one extroverted type.

It is Asymmetrical meaning that partners affect each other unequally where one partner, by default, gets the "short end of the stick" and ends up under the other's influence while largely being unaware of it.

It is also Information Based meaning that the conscious attitudes of one partner "talks" to the conscious attitudes of the other. This has a minor subconscious impact since the exchange of information is repulsive by nature.

Finally, a Large Psychological Distance is fostered whereby the relationship consists of one rational (j) and one irrational (p) type whom, for the most part, have different rhythms, different moods, and different reactions in the same situation.

An example of relations of supervision, comparing one INTj – Analyst in Supervisor role with one ENFp – Psychologist in Supervisee role.

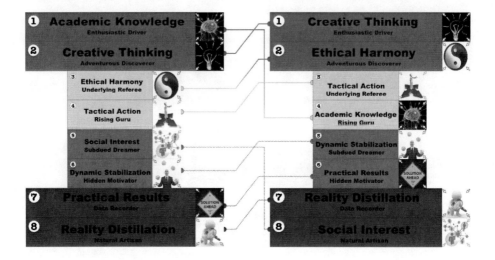

**Comments:**

- Both partners have the same attitudes existing in their conscious area.
- Both partners have the same attitudes existing in their subconscious area.
- The Enthusiastic Driver attitude of the Supervisor is the Rising Guru attitude (shyness) of the Supervisee.
- Accepting attitudes correspond with producing attitudes and vice-versa.

As we can see from the table above, the attitudes of the Supervisee diagonally correspond in a downward direction from right to left with the Supervisor except for the Rising Guru attitude which is the main reason behind this asymmetrical relationship.

The Supervisor, by default of his strong Enthusiastic Driver attitude, is in an apparently superior position towards the Supervisee which can and will lead to having certain repercussions for both although let's bear in mind that it is the Supervisee who has been dealt the proverbial "short end of the stick".

The conscious and strong, accepting attitude of the INTj (Academic Knowledge) is the conscious and weak producing attitude of the ENFp. This results in one type's strength making vulnerable the other type's weakness. A supervisor may seldom be aware of how they may be influencing the weak, underdeveloped area of a supervisee in their presence.

Relations of supervision are information based and thus repulsive. In the presence of an ENFp, an INTj, by default, fits into the role of "intellectual protector" due to the hierarchical discrepancy between AK attitudes. From a supervisor perspective, a supervisee's shortcomings are detectable and can be easily patronised and undervalued at first. As the relationship progresses a somewhat expected phenomenon occurs, the supervisee, realising their defenceless weakness will likely attempt to fight for supremacy, seeking to prove their worth. Unfortunately, while their efforts may appear noble, the supervisor wins by default on account of their superior ego. For example, ENFp's usually seek out the INTj's intellect as a pillar of strength though however much they develop their character relations are still asymmetrical and thus remains a considerable psychological distance.

Since every type can have relations with supervision, everyone, figuratively speaking can be boss and be bossed by another type equating to the four loops of supervision as follows:

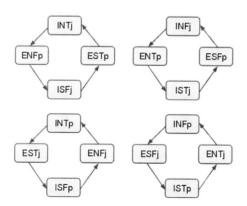

In conclusion, relations of supervision can be summarised as being one of protector and protected – a bit like a child and their guardian.

## RELATIONS OF BENEFIT
### "LOOKS LIKE YOUR INNER-CHILD IS LOST, CAN I HELP?"

## AT A GLANCE
Relations of Benefit involve two aspects where the Beneficiary seeks to offer advice to the weak area of the Benefactor, and the Benefactor is poorly receptive to the Beneficiary's advice.

It is Monoverted meaning that the relationship consists of two introverted or two extroverted types.

It is Asymmetrical meaning that partners affect each other unequally where one partner, by default, gets the "short end of the stick" and ends up under the other's influence while largely being unaware of it.

It is also Energy Based meaning that the conscious attitudes of one partner "talks" to the subconscious attitudes of the other. This has a major subconscious impact since the exchange of information is attractive by nature.

Finally, a Large Psychological Distance is fostered whereby the relationship consists of one rational (j) and one irrational (p) type whom, for the most part, have different rhythms, different moods, and different reactions in the same situation.

An example of relations of benefit, comparing one INTj – Analyst in the role of Benefactor with one ISTp – Craftsman in the role of Beneficiary.

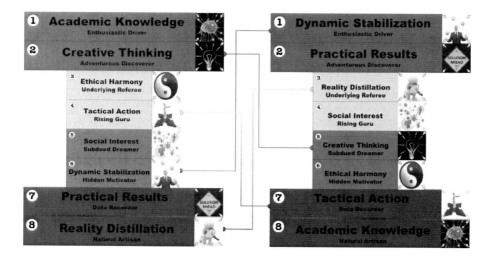

**Comments:**
- All conscious attitudes of both partners are found in the subconscious area of the other.
- The Enthusiastic Driver (1st) attitude of the Beneficiary is the Hidden Motivator (6th) attitude of the Benefactor.
- Accepting attitudes correspond with producing attitudes and vice-versa.

As we can see from the table above, the attitudes of the Benefactor diagonally compare in a downward direct from left to right with the Beneficiary except the orientations are reversed a bit like extinguishing relations.

Unlike relations of supervision which can get unassumingly patronising these relationships are perhaps more fruitful and being energy based it is attractive.

The Beneficiary with his strong Enthusiastic Driver attitude sets his mind on offering advice to the weak and subconscious Super-Id conscience of the Benefactor.

As we may know by now, the Hidden Motivator attitude is kind of like the inner-child that doesn't like to admit that it needs or wants support, and so the Benefactor usually provides little or no feedback where the Beneficiary might expect it.

The Beneficiary has drawn the proverbial "short end of the stick" where he often views the Benefactor as a significant person who he can get something from that no one else can provide thus an automatic difference in respect towards him. The Benefactor as if aware of this may not understand what the Beneficiary needs and may find him overwhelming in the beginning. The Benefactor is thus a spiritual leader about the Beneficiary whose ego is seldom appreciated. For example, a Beneficiary can sometimes present themselves to the Benefactor, who wonders what they want.

Since every type can have relations with benefit, everyone, figuratively speaking can be a spiritual guide and have a spiritual guide thus equating to the four loops of benefaction as follows:

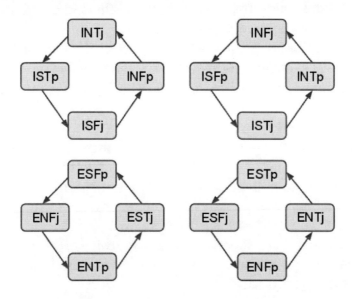

In conclusion, relations of benefit can be summarised as one of spiritual guidance and spiritually guided which becomes active when the Benefactor has something to offer the Beneficiary.

# PART THREE: SMALL GROUPS

In parts one and two, we explored the sixteen psychological types and the relationships between them - individually. From this point on I will refer to the types as sociological types or simply socio-types. To complete the global puzzle, I would like you to appreciate the relations between socio-types collectively where together they will either share what I call "comparable themes" or "observable effects" depending on the members present.

Comparable themes relate four socio-types together that collectively have an underlying consciousness behind their actions. Observable effects are slightly different as I describe four socio-types together that will have less in common by default thus leading to predictably altered states of being sometimes healthy and unhealthy for those involved.

Small groups will come in useful as a broad set of psychoanalytic tools for the practical psychologist who needs to identify and verify socio-types in real-time. For example, in a session with a client you would run through a (mental) checklist of the various groups you think the person appears to fit into. You may even ask specific "control questions" to narrow down the possibilities. However as your rote mastery of this art increases, you will be more in tune with your new social senses with a useful appreciation of who you 'are' dealing with which raises the question of how you will negotiate with them in various endeavours.

The identification of small groups is not new; social trends have been observed for centuries since at least from the times of Plato and Aristotle who were amongst the first to notice and document their prevalent "four types of character".

The small groups I'm about to present have only actually been exposed during the latter 20th century due to advancements and renewed interest in the social sciences. So to show you at a glance how much more comprehensive this gets I will present a total of fourteen small groups, and that's not to say there aren't more but simply the amount I felt relevant to this edition.

## COMPARABLE THEMES

### QUADRAS

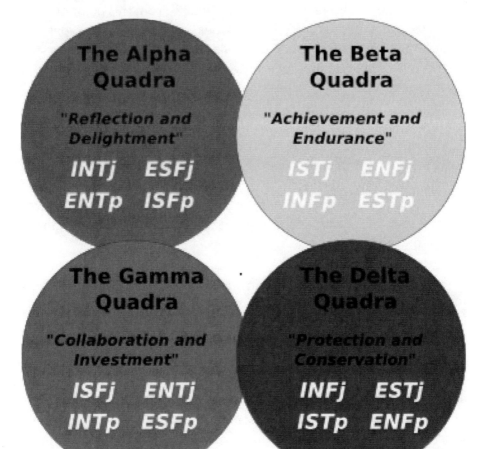

The Alpha Quadra

"Reflection and Delightment"

INTj    ESFj

ENTp    ISFp

The Beta Quadra

"Achievement and Endurance"

ISTj    ENFj

INFp    ESTp

The Gamma Quadra

"Collaboration and Investment"

ISFj    ENTj

INTp    ESFp

The Delta Quadra

"Protection and Conservation"

INFj    ESTj

ISTp    ENFp

A Quadra is a set of four socio-types whom collectively share compatible social dynamics that makes their interactions highly comfortable with an abundance of understanding making for psycho-therapeutic indulgences, by default. This also provides them with an abundance of energy where each member has enough differing abilities that will quite easily support and complement the others leading to high working capacities in mostly harmonious operating environments.

A Quadra collectively represents to me "a shared comfort-zone" and only one-quarter of our society's complete make-up. This means that without appreciations of other quadras one cannot achieve true self-actualization as to become a 'rounded person' without an effort to learn about other quadras and their outlooks on health, happiness, romance and prosperity. For this reason, the Quadra is acknowledged as being the leading 'umbrella group'.

The naming convention of the quadras borrows letters from the Greek alphabet and is merely for classification purposes only and should not be taken as some social hierarchy. As with individual socio-types, it is only one's subjective perception that can give value to the rhetorical questions of "what's the best socio-type to be?" and "what's the best Quadra to belong to?".

In regards to the flow of information I will say there is, in fact, a value creation cycle similar to that in software development where alpha represents the pre-development and prototyping stage, beta approximates to the in-development and testing phase, gamma signifies the release candidate and finalizing stage, and lastly, delta marks the gold or packaged stage.

I have summarised this cycle of values as "Alpha Innovation" round to "Beta Refinement" round to "Gamma Monetization" round to "Delta Distribution". As a quick example, I can see at a glance how alpha's creative efforts could go under-marketed without gamma's monetization practices. Mix in a touch of beta's artistic proofing with delta's cultural disseminations and we end up with a complete socio-business system for competitive value production.

## Clubs

**The Socials**

*"Sociable People In Tune With Society*

*ISFj    ESFj*

*ESFp    ISFp*

**The Pragmatists**

*"Practical Get Things Done Kind Of People"*

*ISTj    ESTj*

*ESTp    ISTp*

**The Researchers**

*"Rationally Pushing For Human Progress"*

*INTj   ENTj*

*ENTp INTp*

**The Humanitarians**

*"Spiritually Led To Make Your Life Better"*

*INFj    ENFj*

*ENFp    INFp*

A club is a set of four socio-types whom collectively share similar core strengths where each member as a subtype of these similar 'occupational mindsets' can address a problem of related natures in its entirety and thus forming a mastermind group together. Each member will have his or her view on an issue of common interest and thus contributes constructively.

A club collectively represents to me "a laser-targeted focus group" and only one-quarter of the mentalities that makes an entire society workable. This means that without appreciations of other clubs one cannot function accordingly to four human needs which I shall summarise as "living, learning, loving and leaving a legacy". For this reason, the club is usually acknowledged as the small auxiliary group to quadras and is frequently cross-referenced with it.

By default, this small group is weak for actual joint implementation of projects due to different quadra values, individual creative attitudes and resulting styles of work. However with appreciations of each socio-type involved brings to them workable solutions that allow members of the same club to get their acts mainly together combining individual efforts in a way that is comfortable while satisfying and working towards the collective goals of the club.

As with quadras, there is no better/worse club to be in other than in your subjective perceptions based on your current level of personal experience and emotionally-influenced biases. However depending on the context of a situation, problem or issue a particular club may appear better qualified to handle it albeit with scrutiny from other clubs whom may lack the necessary reasoning to trust their judgements.

One of the most prevalent clubs is the 'socials' or SF's whom usually come across to others as sympathetic and friendly generally in tune with 'fashionable society' with a state or quality of behaving socially thus versed in the art of small talk. Another one of the most prevalent clubs are the 'pragmatists' or ST's whom usually have a practical, matter-of-fact way of approaching or assessing situations or of solving problems.

One of the least prevalent clubs is the 'humanitarians' or NF's whom usually come across as enthusiastic and insightful with concerns for helping to improve the welfare and happiness of people. Another one of the least prevalent clubs is the 'researchers' or NT's whom usually come across as logical and ingenious skilled in performing a diligent and systematic inquiry or investigation into a subject to discover or revise facts, theories, applications, etc.

To summarise I will say that 'socials' and 'pragmatists' tend to command most influence on instant gratification subcultures, leisure & fitness, maintaining organisations and social stigmatisations, etc. By contrast, the 'humanitarians' and 'researchers' tend to command the most influence on philosophy, ethics, science, innovation, medicine, business, etc.

## TEMPERAMENTS

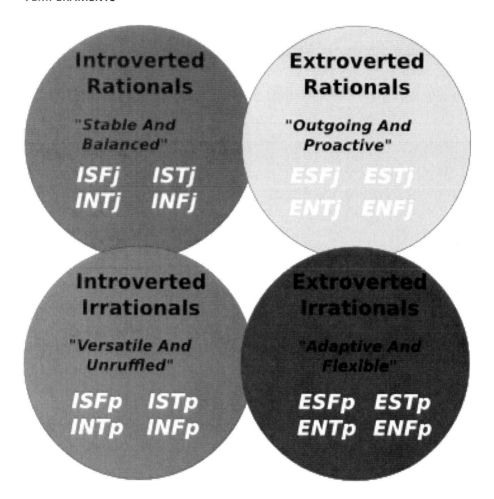

Introverted Rationals

"Stable And Balanced"

ISFj    ISTj
INTj    INFj

Extroverted Rationals

"Outgoing And Proactive"

ESFj    ESTj
ENTj    ENFj

Introverted Irrationals

"Versatile And Unruffled"

ISFp    ISTp
INTp    INFp

Extroverted Irrationals

"Adaptive And Flexible"

ESFp    ESTp
ENTp    ENFp

A temperament group is a set of four socio-types whom collectively share an innate aspect of personality, such as introversion or extroversion which is acknowledged as genetically based whereby influencing overall character, body type, energy levels, stamina, agility, etc.

As you may begin to realise, by deconstructing personality down to its core elements we are slowly yet surely debunking popular myths and stereotypes surrounding wildly misunderstood terms like "introvert" and "extrovert". Originally coined by Carl Jung these terms have more to do with temperaments as we're discussing here than with social needs.

A socio-type has a temperament which begins on the premise the ego was orientated towards behaving introverted or extroverted. We then couple this with whether their dominant attitude is rational (reasoning) or irrational (perceptive). This gives us four subtypes of temperament of "introverted rationals", "introverted irrationals", "extroverted rationals", and "extroverted irrationals".

The introverted rationals (or IJ's) tend to come across as stable and balanced in a social situation, and may appear edgy and stressed in response to any perceived chaos in the environment. The introverted irrationals (or IP's) tend to come across as versatile and unruffled in a social situation, and may appear tend to have sudden mood swings in response to rising stress levels.

The extroverted rationals (or EJ's) tend to come across as outgoing and pro-active doing what they need to get done albeit without deep introspection thus living a hectic lifestyle. The extroverted irrationals (or EP's) tend to come across as adaptable and flexible able to go with the flow in situations that demand it thus comfortable with last-minute excursions.

Hence IJ's live a measured life, the IP's live a leisurely life, the EJ's live a zealous life, and the EP's live a mutable life. IJ's and EJ's both want to get things done definitively and on-time. In contrast, IP's and EP's also want to get things done albeit flexible and untimely. Thus we have a mini-dichotomy between strict and relaxed adherence to project and time management after the initial decision-making of goals and objectives.

STIMULUS

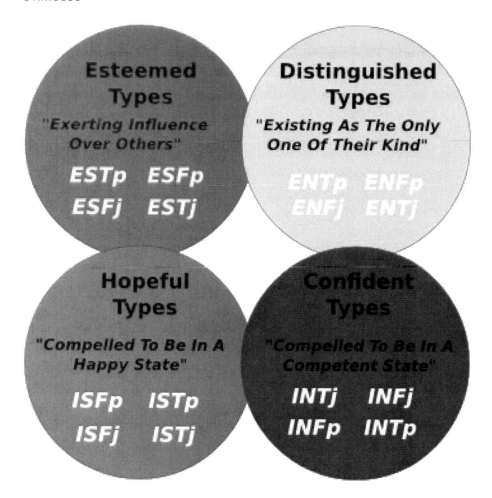

A stimuli group is a set of four socio-types whom collectively share the same dominant or automatic attitudes that may have an impact or influence on their overall actions. This will, in turn, have a side effect on the rest of the social system that may further elicit or influence physiological or psychological activities or responses in others.

The stimulus of each socio-type represents to me "a personal call-to-action" and mainly comes from a person's ego or id which are both strong, and conscious or unconscious respectively. The only difference is how well they are understood thus leading to a degree of self-control for each. By default remember that the dominant attitude is used arrogantly without any shyness while the automatic attitude (as the name suggests) gets used as a skill taken for granted.

In the modern day age of social media with the likes of Twitter and Facebook, it doesn't take a genius to figure out a person's stimulus based on the kind of updates they post. From the girl who can't stop telling the world how she is attending the next big party this weekend to the guy who can't stop telling us how the New World Order is coming, to the philosopher who usually says something inspirational, to the person who seeks practical advice, and so on.

Esteemed types (or ES's) are often compelled by having a high reputation, honour or esteem, exerting influence because of their high status. Distinguished types (or EN's) are often compelled by existing as the only one or as the sole example; single; solitary in type or characteristics. Hopeful types (IS's) are often compelled by a contented state of being happy, healthy and prosperous. Confident types (IN's) are often compelled by a realistic confidence in one's judgement, ability, power, etc.

Hence the ES's attempt to command respect from their peers (even when they have little to be actually recognised for), and the EN's attempt to create a unique persona with the visage of a local celebrity (even if it means embarrassing themselves on occasion). In addition the IS's try to maintain a controlled balance in their lives (although periodically to the irritation of others when it gets too measured), and the IN's try to achieve their own salvation in life independently of authority (even if it means taking risks in new lines of thought and facing an abundance of cynicism).

**ARGUMENTATIONS**

An argumentation group is a set of four socio-types whom collectively share the same dominant and accruing attitudes that are concerned primarily with reaching conclusions through logical or ethical reasoning i.e. claims based on business or social perspectives.

The argumentation of each socio-type represents to me "a preferred approach to a business task or social situation" and involves the simultaneous use of two strong attitudes, one from the conscious and one from the subconscious mind. This will go on to explain why people throughout history may have been billed as "the millionaire messiah who helped get lots of other businesses off the ground" and "the super-nanny who taught a generation how to handle their children properly", etc.

Restructurers (or TP's) are usually focused on changing, altering, or restoring the structure of. Guardians (or FJ's) are often focused on guarding, watching over, protecting or preserving. Constructors (or TJ's) are often focused on creating by systematically arranging ideas or terms. Diplomats (or FP's) are usually tactful and skilful in managing delicate situations, handling people, etc.

Hence the TP's tend to follow the mantra of Voltaire, who distilled that "Originality is nothing but judicious imitation. The most original writers borrowed one from another". The FJ's tend to follow the mantra of Eisenhower who said: "Leadership is the art of getting someone else to do something you want to be done because he wants to do it". The TJ's tend to follow the mantra of Mason Cooley who proclaimed "Mistakes are the only universal form of originality". Lastly, the FP's tend to follow the mantra of Studs Terkel, who affirmed "I want, of course, peace, grace, and beauty. How do you do that? You work for it".

## SALACITIES

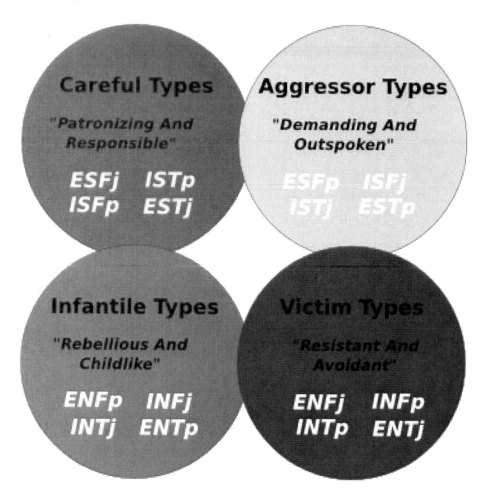

A salacity group is a set of four socio-types whom collectively share a mix of the same ego and id block attitudes that will account for specific lustful desires in and from their interactions with others i.e. selfish advances/retreats that heed conditional reciprocations (or else).

The salacity of each socio-type represents to me "a deep-rooted expectation of how others should respond to their adult-like or inner-child needs" and involves the simultaneous dominance of all strong conscious and subconscious attitudes in the psyche. This explains the prevalent social trends between those who appear to either have patronising or assertive pseudo-authoritarianism versus those who have rebelliousness or resistance to any direct forms of pseudo-authoritarianism.

By default I find that society has either a peaceful complement or hostile conflict between those who think they know best and thus attempt to bestow advice and command others versus those who protest against these "self-appointed godparents of the world" and defensively play hard to get. This explains why many budding entrepreneurs will continue to face a world of patronisations which either leads to defeat or prosperity (when interpreted in the context of 'reverse psychology' where cynicism is just praise expressed irrationally).

The "careful types" (with consciously strong Dynamic Stabilisation attitudes) come pre-packaged with their primary mentality that they automatically know what is best for others (like a zealous parent). In a quasi-identical way, the "aggressor types" (with consciously strong Tactical Action attitudes) come pre-packaged with their primordial mentality that others will submit to their will (like a zealous supervisor).

In response to the above, the "victim types" (with consciously strong Reality Distillation attitudes) adopt their chief defensive mindset that others must earn their genuine respect (like a rare and valuable trophy). Infantile types (with consciously strong Creative Thinking attitudes) by quasi-identical comparison adopt their first delinquent mindset that others can only have and receive their friendship once they respect their personal boundaries.

Hence I believe this to be one of the most important small groups because it gets to the roots of selfishness and is a useful axiom in appreciating compatibility between socio-types in one's professional and personal lives. I also find that it debunks the oversimplified myth that "extroverts are politicians, introverts are leaders" because I can now say it is more accurate to re-frame that as "careful and aggressor types are politicians; victim and infantile types are leaders".

### PHONETICS

A phonetic group is a set of four socio-types whom collectively share a mix of similar ego and id block attitudes (though not identical to the ones in the Salacity groups) that will account for various forms of articulation although usually about vocal sounds and corresponding to pronunciation.

The phonetics of each socio-type represent to me "a preferred method of communication in speech, writing, and resulting action" and involves the simultaneous usage of the strong conscious and subconscious attitudes. This small group works in direct conjunction with Salacities to explain for example, how each "careful type" has their corresponding articulation which not only produces yet another subtype to watch out for but another variable in how a specific socio-type of that subgroup may attempt to bestow their parent-like advice.

By default, there is a stereotypical expectation that women should come across sincere and passionate towards life and each other while men should come across cool and firm towards their career and getting things done. Of course, the trouble with any stereotype is that it doesn't account for the fact that reality is just a wee bit different to that over-simplified idea.

The "melodramatic types" (with extroverted temperaments and strong ethical attitudes) come across to others as usually dramatic and excited about something whether it be a romantic interest, their current hobbies or their career aspirations, etc. The "righteous types" (with introverted temperaments and strong ethical attitudes) come across to others as usually genuine and up-front about their intentions towards others and their personal issues.

The "intrepid types" (with extroverted temperaments and strong logical attitudes) come across to others as usually no-nonsense and purposeful in negotiating through what they want thus making things happen. The "placid types" (with introverted temperaments and strong logical attitudes) come across to others as usually cool-headed and emotionally detached undisturbed by most situations unless antagonised by more hot-blooded people.

Lastly, I have concluded that socio-types within the phonetic groups share common propensities toward specific personality disorders when left unchecked following their default paths of least resistance. At their unhealthiest states of being the "melodramatic types" will correspond with Histrionics (excessive emotional expressions), the "righteous types" will correspond with Avoidance (hypersensitivity to criticism), the "intrepid types" will correspond with Narcissism (admiration-seeking behaviours), and the "placid types" will correspond with Schizoidism (disinterest in social relationships).

## OBSERVABLE EFFECTS

The groups in this section have some measurable effect on each other. For example, with enough time spent within a particular group made up of specific psychological types one may experience changes emotionally and therefore physically as a result.

### SQUARES

A square group is a set of four socio-types made up of complementary relations from two distinct quadras whom will experience the phenomenon of 'spontaneous relaxation' when brought together, kind of like a double-duality environment that provides a very comfortable vacation from real-life.

The square group represents to me "a dual-action relief group ideal for alleviating tensions" providing the social dynamics that restores psychological equilibrium quicker than a single complementary relationship would.

The alpha and delta quadras align to give two sets of complementary relations consisting of four irrational (p) or four rational(j) socio-types each. The ENTp-ISFp pair plus the ENFp-ISTp pair make up a square group, and the ESFj-INTj pair plus the ESTj-INFj pair make a square group.

The beta and gamma quadras align to give another two sets of complementary relations following the same rules as above. The ESTp-INFp pair plus the ESFp-INTp pair make up a square group, and the ENFj-ISTj pair plus the ENTj-ISFj pair make up a square group.
The four irrational (p) socio-types in a square group will share complementary, semi-complementary and kindred relations between them. By contrast, the four rational (j) socio-types will share complementary, mirage and business relationships between them.

Hence square groups contain all the fundamental social dynamics required that encourages liberations from neuroses with a hint of emphatic and proactive life management. I would describe the experience as like going on an exclusive retreat to recuperate in a psychologically comfortable environment and then laying down plans for future actions.

## HEALTH

A health group is a set of four socio-types made up of irrational (p) or rational (j) members of two specific clubs whom essentially transfuse each other's psychic energy and rejuvenate themselves.

The health group represents to me "a parasitism of recovery" where each member figuratively feeds off the mental vitality of the other members until they equalise their physiological outputs.

According to medical studies after 1.5 – 2 hours of interaction all members of these health groups feel better and demonstrate normalisation of objective characteristics such as blood pressure, pulse rate and breathing rates.

The researchers and humanitarians clubs consist of four irrational (p) socio-types. The socials and pragmatists clubs align comprised of four irrational (p) socio-types). The humanitarian and socials clubs align consisting of four rational (j) socio-types. The researchers and pragmatists clubs include four rational (j) socio-types.

In each health group, the members will share relations of extinguishment, Mirage and kindred. This explains why when these socio-types come together they will find a way to calm collectively down sharing the same rhythmic needs.

## BOUQUETS

A bouquet group is a set of four socio-types made up of socio-types with equal temperaments whom mainly graze each other's psychic energy and deplete themselves.

The bouquet group represents to me "a parasitism of contamination" where each member figuratively feeds off the mental vitality of the other members in an unstable way to their eventual detriment.

According to observation, a deterioration of health comes from too much stimulation or resonance (energy vibration) directed towards each other's weak areas in their respective psyches.

In each bouquet group, the members will share relations of kindred, super-ego and business. It is interesting to note that kindred relationships get another mention here as well as in the health groups. However, we have to remember that members are affected by a whole group after 'x' amount of time which creates the conditions for further medical studies to be carried out.

## PARAGONS

A paragon group is a set of four socio-types made up of a ring of supervision where each member is simultaneously the supervisor and supervisee relation to an adjacent member.

The Paragon group represents to me "the neurotic path of most resistance to personal development" where each member has their corresponding archetype in the form of their supervisor. In other words, a supreme example of their conscious censored weakness in another socio-type thus producing intense neuroses and tense relations in which members are incapable of any joint activity.

In each paragon group, the members will share relations of supervision and a super-ego relationship which acts to ease the tensions slightly where a supervisee of one member gets some 'balance of power' by also being the supervisor of another.

In conclusion, the paragon group has the most to learn and gain from their interactions with each other albeit requiring the most effort to compete unconsciously for each other's egotistic strengths.

## ACOLYTES

An acolyte group is a set of four socio-types made up of a ring of benefaction where each member is simultaneously the benefactor and beneficiary relation to an adjacent member.

The acolyte group represents to me "the undemanding path of least resistance to personal development" where each has their corresponding 'spiritual advisor' in the form of their beneficiary. In other words, a friendly companion who respects their benefactor enough to freely offers them advice via direct articulation and indirect actions.

In each acolyte group, the members will share relations of benefaction and a super-ego relationship which acts to distract the beneficiaries and take pressure off of their corresponding benefactor thus acting as a kind of release valve that regulates any over-amenability.

In conclusion, the acolyte group has the least to learn and gain from their interactions with each other albeit requiring the least effort to take onboard any new advice circulating.

## ADDITIONAL GROUPS

A few more noteworthy groups that I didn't feel belonged in the previous sections as they don't necessarily correlate with a partner or contrary group thus making them each standalone. I will cover the kind of expectations specific socio-types tend to have with regards to their education needs and how they deal with periods of stress.

### PEDAGOGUES

A pedagogue group is a set of four socio-types whom collectively share preferred styles of being taught/coached with expectations for any recognition sought on completion of a teaching/coaching programme.

The pedagogics of each socio-type represents to me "an inherent philosophy of learning that must ideally be adhered to if they're to benefit truly from their education" where specific methods of tuition and coaching will ensure the best results while believing that everyone learns the same way is flawed.

For over two hundred years the learning philosophy of constructivism has been around except not widely implemented or accepted by most educational institutions today. The mass of students still gets subjected to traditional learning styles that haven't changed significantly for years and have always favoured quite simply, those who don't think while denouncing those who do. Instead of fostering the next generation of creative thinkers, authors, artists and entrepreneurs, students are just viewed as 'blank slates' to be etched onto, and there is a simple reason for this, it works for the needs of the majority.

The "traditional learners" expect to follow a straight course leading to a recognised qualification or certification at the end that should guarantee employment based on the closed-mindedness of mainstream employers who recognise traditional awards like a bachelor's degree. The "liberal learners" expect to follow a non-linear course leading to any qualification or certification at the end that should guarantee employment based on the open-mindedness of mainstream employers who recognise exceptional achievements like an associate's degree.

The "utopian learners" expect to study and research ethical problems and gain recognition for their ability to offer solutions to receive appropriate respect. The "conceptual learners" hope to study and research logical problems and gain recognition for their capacity to provide solutions to receive appropriate honours.

In conclusion, I found that most of the world's richest tended to fall under the last subgroup category for the reason that its members have minimal to gain from pure academia because their brains are already wired for it i.e. they already value life-long learning, by default. Is it any wonder that some of the wealthiest people were high school dropouts? No, they were simply "conceptual learners" who had their pedagogic requirements misunderstood and that's before anyone investigated their measurable socio-type.

## SUSCEPTIBILITIES

A susceptibility group is a set of four socio-types whom collectively share a common stress behaviour brought about as a result of a contingent liability i.e. when an instinctual need goes awry a primitive contingency plan goes into effect.

The susceptibility of each socio-type represents to me "a predictable response to the environment which either results in a cyclothymic or schizothymic reaction". This accounts for the social trend of individuals predisposed to depressive and hypomanic mood disorders, and those who cycle between sensitivity and insensitivity as a form of social protection.

I tend to find in a society that people unconsciously set themselves up for disappointment and failure without understanding why and how repeated attempts at a similar level thinking are not necessarily going to solve the problem. The conditional stress behaviours mostly explain how people react to disappointment or increasing social tension.

The "dysphoric types" are predisposed to getting a case of the blues if they lose a sense of belonging in society hence why they tend to populate organisations, clubs, bars, community groups, etc. The "frenzy types" are predisposed to over-excitement as a way of steering themselves towards pleasure and away from potential pain hence why they tend to enjoy work that provides a lot of flexible compensation to pay for their frequent social excursions.

The "emotional types" are predisposed to appearing too sensitive to the environment and will not tolerate too much perceived discord in others hence why they can take things to heart too quickly leading to poor decisions. The "callous types" are predisposed to appearing too insensitive towards the environment where they have thick skins and the final say as to what they allow to affect them socially.

Hence there are a few underlying conditions that govern what creates stress for an individual. From a need to belong or indulge leading to disappointment if say socialising doesn't lead to what they wanted, to escaping into one's mind as a defence mechanism from the increased perceived annoyance or discord of others.

## CONCLUSION

I trust that you have benefited from reading this book and that it has assisted your personal and social development. In my opinion, there are two truths we can learn from the ancient Stoics:

"Live by nature" and "Live in accordance with your nature".

In the context of Socionics, I believe that an understanding of psychological or socio-type, together with an appreciation of the inter-type relations can help people better understand each other and lead to more harmonious living.

# APPENDICES

## APPENDIX A

The following table summarises the inter-type relations by their attributes:

| Relation | Hetroverted | Symmetrical | Energy-Based | Rhythmical |
|---|---|---|---|---|
| Duality | Yes | Yes | Yes | Yes |
| Activity | No | Yes | Yes | No |
| Mirror | Yes | Yes | No | No |
| Identity | No | Yes | No | Yes |
| Kindred | No | Yes | No | Yes |
| Partial-Duality | Yes | Yes | Yes | Yes |
| Extinguishing | Yes | Yes | Yes | Yes |
| Super-Ego | No | Yes | No | Yes |
| Business | No | Yes | No | Yes |
| Mirage | Yes | Yes | Yes | Yes |
| Quasi-Identity | No | Yes | Yes | No |
| Conflicting | Yes | Yes | No | No |
| Supervision | Yes | No | No | No |
| Benefit | No | No | Yes | No |

## APPENDIX B

The following table summarises the conditions for "optimal relations" as follows:

- Condition One: Information elements that are accepting in one type must be accepting in the other type;
- Condition Two: Information elements that are producing in one type must be producing in the other type;
- Condition Three: Information elements that are conscious of one type must be subconscious in the other type;
- Condition Four: Information elements that are weak of one type must be strong in the other type;

Please note: Conditions one and two are not mutually exclusive and will be combined in the following table. To list the inter-type relations in "most optimal" order, I had to provide a weighting for each condition. To keep things simple, conditions three and four will take precedence over conditions one and two.

| Relation | Condition One/Two | Condition Three | Condition Four |
|---|---|---|---|
| Duality | Yes (4 of 4) | Yes (4 of 4) | Yes (4 of 4) |
| Activity | No | Yes (4 of 4) | Yes (4 of 4) |
| Partial-Duality | Yes (4 of 4) | Yes (4 of 4) | Yes (2 of 4) |
| Mirage | Yes (4 of 4) | Yes (4 of 4) | Yes (2 of 4) |
| Benefit | No | Yes (2 of 4) | Yes (2 of 4) |
| Super-Ego | Yes (4 of 4) | No | Yes (4 of 4) |
| Extinguishing | Yes (4 of 4) | Yes (4 of 4) | No |
| Quasi-Identity | No | Yes (4 of 4) | No |
| Kindred | Yes (4 of 4) | No | Yes (2 of 4) |
| Business | Yes (4 of 4) | No | Yes (2 of 4) |
| Conflicting | No | No | Yes (4 of 4) |
| Supervision | No | No | Yes (1 of 4) |
| Identity | Yes (4 of 4) | No | No |
| Mirror | No | No | No |

# RECOMMENDED RESOURCES

- The Introvert Advantage: How to Thrive in an Extrovert World, Marti Olsen Laney, ISBN 0761123695 (2002)
- The Undiscovered Self, Carl G. Jung, ISBN 0710077998 (1958)
- Psychological Types, Carl G. Jung, ISBN 0415071771 (1992) (New Edition)

# GLOSSARY OF TERMS

Ambiversion - A personality trait including the qualities of both introversion and extroversion.

Ambiverted attitude - A tendency to feel comfortable with groups and enjoy social interactions and equally relish time alone, away from the crowd.

Archetype - An ideal example of a type.

Dichotomy - A division of a whole into two constituent parts usually of opposite extremes.

Dyad - Two individuals or units of the Socion regarded as a pair, often associated with the eight relations of duality.

Ego - The most conscious area of the psyche, in essence, your 'self' that the world sees first before getting to know the complete 'you'.

Ethics - A rational mode of reasoning based on moral values.

Extrospective - In essence, to seek out external help in examining your sensory and perceptual experiences for solutions to any self-made problems.

Extrospective introvert - An introverted person who seeks out external means or help to achieve something in the 'real world' (also see extroverted attitude).

Extroversion - The interest in or behaviour directed toward others or one's environment rather than oneself.

Extrovert - An extroverted person.

Extroverted attitude - A tendency to act energetic, enthusiastic, action-orientated, talkative, and assertive.

Id - The most unconscious area of the psyche, in essence, the instinctual 'self' which the ego keeps under control for 'you' and everybody else's sakes.

Instrumentalism - A philosophy that views ideas and theories as useful tools with little or nothing to do with correctly depicting reality, merely serving to explain effectively and predict phenomena.

Introspective - In essence, to look within and examine your sensory and perceptual experiences for solutions to self-made problems.

Introspective extrovert - An extroverted person who looks within for the knowledge to achieve something in the 'real world' (also see introverted attitude).

Introversion - The tendency to direct one's thoughts and feelings toward oneself.

Introvert - An introverted person.

Introverted attitude - A tendency to act quiet, low-key, deliberate, and disengaged from the social world.

Intuition - An irrational (or perceiving) function to interpret the world through the interpretation of signs and use of the mind's eye.

Logic - A rational mode of reasoning that concerns us with 'truth' and how we can prove or disprove the existence of these so-called 'truths'.

Psychology - The science that deals with mental processes and behaviour.

Quadra - A rational and irrational pair of dyads that share relations of duality, identity, activation and mirror.

Sensation - An irrational (or perceiving) function to interpret the world according to the five senses of sight, smell, hearing, taste and touch.

Social Psychology - The branch of psychology concerned with people and their relationships with others as individuals, in groups and with society as a whole.

Socion - A complete set of four quadras or eight dyads making up the sixteen types.

Socionics - a theory of information processing and personality type, distinguished by its information model of the psyche (called Model A) and a model of interpersonal relations.

Stereotype - A generalisation, usually exaggerated or oversimplified and often offensive, that is used to describe or distinguish a group

Super-ego - The medium between the ego and id, in essence, the moralist who keeps law and order for 'you'.

11767992R00122